20TH CENTURY ROCK AND ROLL

POP

Dave Thompson

WATCH FOR THE REST OF THE SERIES

A GUIDE TO THE ARTISTS WHO MADE THE CENTURY'S GREATEST ROCK MUSIC

20th CENTURY ROCK AND ROLL

A COLLECTOR'S GUIDE PUBLISHING SERIES

Psychedelia	ISBN 1-896522-40-8
Alternative Music	ISBN 1-896522-19-X
Progressive Rock	ISBN 1-896522-20-3
Heavy Metal	ISBN 1-896522-47-5
Pop Music	ISBN 1-896522-25-4
Punk Rock	ISBN 1-896522-27-0
Glam Rock	ISBN 1-896522-26-2
Women In Rock	ISBN 1-896522-29-7

For ordering information see our web site at
www.cgpublishing.com

We acknowledge the financial support of the Government of Canada through
the Book Publishing Industry Development Program for our publishing activities.
Published by Collector's Guide Publishing Inc., Box 62034, Burlington, Ontario, Canada, L7R 4K2
Printed and bound in Canada
20th Century Rock and Roll - Pop
by Dave Thompson
ISBN 1-896522-25-4

20TH CENTURY ROCK AND ROLL

POP

Dave Thompson

Table Of Contents

Before We Start . . .

Pop is ephemeral, pop is of the moment, and pure pop has so little to do with "personalities" that for the first five years of modern musical history (and indeed for another five after that), even stringing two or three big hits together was a miraculous achievement. The accomplishments of Elvis Presley in the US and Cliff Richard in the UK not withstanding, it wasn't until the Beatles emerged as a genuine force in 1963-64 that the notion of pop music as a sustainable career even begin to dawn on most performers (songwriters, managers and publishers, of course, had long since figured it out), and even then it was another year or two before the effects of that dawning truly began to make themselves felt.

Of course, the one (or two)-off smash hit remained a power in the land; which means that the arrangement of this book was problematic right from the start. Any poll of the top pop groups of the century — even once the actual definition of the term "pop" has been roughly decided upon — is going to be weighted so heavily in favor of the One Hit Wonders that we could use that as a subtitle. But to do so would be committing a horrible injustice because we'd be ignoring the careers which were wrapped around those solitary hits, and the men and minds who were often linked to the best of them.

The American bubblegum team of Kasenatz Katz may never have scored a hit in their own right, but as writers and producers they equipped the late 1960's with a soundtrack which remains as vibrant as any other act of the era. Carole Bayer, Carole King, Don Kirshner, Graham Gouldman, Jonathan King, Tony Burroughs, Tony Dante, Tony Orlando, Maurice Starr, Micky Most — again and again as we leaf through both the written and unwritten history of pop music, these names crop up (far more than the people who performed them) as often as the musicians with whom those songs are best associated.

Much of this book, then, details not just the top pop groups, but also the top pop producers, the top pop session men, the top pop entrepreneurs, and finally, the top pop songs of the century. To make it all accessible to the reader, this book is organized by hit songs and their artists in chronological order.

Before we begin, we must ask the question: "what is pop?" It's such a limitless term that sometimes only success (screaming, hysterical, obsessive, adulatory, insane-beyond-one's-wildest-dreams success) can be considered the defining factor — the term "pop", after all, is simply an abbreviation of the term "popular music." Some years it was Rock and Roll that was most popular, other years it was bubblegum, etc. And in any given year there was more than one style of music that was popular with the listening (and buying) public. But there were few that got the kids screaming. And those are the few which we called pop.

But that, surely, is far more explanation than you need. It is, after all, only pop music. And if there's one lesson to be learned from listening to all these groups (and songs and producers and session men and entrepreneurs), it's that pop music can be a lot of different things — more things than you can imagine. And finally, if we acknowledge that for every artist included here, there's at least one or two more who could and/or should have been included, then hopefully somebody else might agree with the following list.

The Captain Sooper Dooper Rock And Roll Hall Of Pop And Bubblegum Fame

These are the records which justify the contents of this book.

1959: Tommy Facenda — *High School USA*
1963: Cliff Richard — *Summer Holiday*
1965: Herman's Hermits — *Mrs. Brown You've Got A Lovely Daughter*
1966: The Walker Brothers — *The Sun Ain't Gonna Shine*
1966: Tommy James And The Shondells — *Hanky Panky*
1966: The Monkees — *I'm A Believer*
1967: Dave Dee, Dozy, Beaky, Mick And Tich — *Zabadak*
1967: The Herd — *From The Underworld*
1967: The Bee Gees — *Massachussetts*
1967: The Cowsills — *The Rain, The Park And Other Things*
1967: The Music Explosion — *Little Bit O'Soul*
1968: The Ohio Express — *Yummy Yummy Yummy*
1968: The 1910 Fruitgum Company — *Simon Says*
1969: Tommy Roe — *Dizzy*
1969: The Archies — *Sugar Sugar*
1969: The Jackson Five — *I Want You Back*
1970: The Pipkins — *Gimme Dat Ding*
1970: Hotlegs — *Neanderthal Man*
1970: The Partridge Family — *I Think I Love You*
1971: The Osmonds — *One Bad Apple*
1971: The Carpenters — *Superstar*
1972: Bubblerock — *Satisfaction*
1973: Tony Orlando And Dawn — *Tie A Yellow Ribbon Round The Ole Oak Tree*
1973: The Defranco Family, featuring Tony Defranco — *Heartbeat, It's A Lovebeat*
1974: Carl Douglas — *Kung Fu Fighting*
1974: ABBA — *Waterloo*
1975: The Bay City Rollers — *Saturday Night*
1976: John Travolta — *Let Her In*
1983: New Edition — *Candy Girl*
1988: New Kids On The Block — *You Got It (The Right Stuff)*
1989: Milli Vanilli — *Baby Don't Forget My Number*
1995: Take That — *Back For Good*
1996: The Spice Girls — *Wannabe*
1997: Babylon Zoo — *Spaceman*
1997: Hanson — *MMM Bop*
1998: Gala — *Freed From Desire*
1998: All Saints — *Never Ever*
1998: The Backstreet Boys — *As Long As You Love Me*
1998: 'N Sync — *You Drive Me Crazy*

And finally — The Eurovision Song Contest — without which none of this would have been necessary.

~ Introduction ~
We All Got High On Bubblegum

History has not recorded who first applied the term Bubblegum to Pop Music. Gum itself had been around since the early 1900's when one Frank H. Fleer marketed a gooey substance called "Blibber Blubber." Certain teething problems (such as the difficulty encountered trying to blow a bubble that didn't immediately stick to your face) took 20 years to iron out, but when "Dubble Bubble Gum" was introduced around 1928, it was an immediate success.

In wartime Europe, gum was up there with dairy chocolate and silk stockings in every sexually active GI's basic survival kit. In Borneo, headhunters kidnapped a diplomat and demanded Dubble Bubble as ransom. And in 1950's America, a mouthful of gum was as vital to the teenage revolution as any leather jacket, Elvis quiff or James Dean sneer.

In 1955, The Scholastic Label, A Subsidiary Of Folkways, released 33 SKIP ROPE GAMES, an LP recorded on the streets of Chicago by folkie Pete Seeger, consisting of the rhymes children chanted as they skipped. One such rhyme was *Bubblegum*, and a decade later, the progenitors of the then imminent musical genre might well have had a copy of the chant alongside the piano when they first began piecing together the ingredients they required.

> Standing on the corner
> Chewing bubblegum
> Along came a little boy
> And asked for some
> No, you little boy
> No, you dirty bum
> You can't have any
> Of my bubblegum

The ingredients were gathered slowly. A hint of *The Nitty Gritty*, a dash of *Loop De Loop*, a sprinkling of *Yellow Submarine*. Elsewhere, Richard Berry's archetypical *Louie Louie* riff, arguably the most important noise to emerge from post-Beatle-whipped America, came shrieking out of garageland to proffer a utilitarian beat which, with only the slightest revision, could lift any song out of the Pop Novelty market and into a world all its very own.

The garage scene, which the Kingsmen pioneered and which was to influence and (via the later maneuverings of the Shadows Of Knight et al) then find itself absorbed by Bubblegum, burst out of California and Oregon as an immediate gut reaction to the Beatles' breakthrough. There were few generic links between the pioneers. In the southwest it was the surf sound which predominated, the quintessential harmonies of the Beach Boys and Jan and Dean being diluted into something much muddier only by the new bands' inability to do them properly.

In the north, on the other hand, it was the British Invasion which set the precedents. You'd hear George Harrison's one finger guitar solo on any number of the Fab Four's earliest waxings, compare it with your own struggling melodies and suddenly the realization would dawn — "Hey! I can play that!" And when you found maybe it wasn't quite as easy as it originally appeared, you'd just turn everything up full blast and forget the solos altogether. Then you'd find three or four friends, scrape together a few more instruments, plug them all into the same tinny amplifier and everything else would just fall into place.

That was the great thing about the US garage scene — once you stopped trying to be Clapton or Lennon or Beck, it was easy, it was fun, and it was effective. Even today, the Who's Pete Townshend describes Washington State's The Wailers as one of the greatest bands he has ever heard, but it was the Kingsmen, from Portland, who finally lifted the sound out of the local scene and into the annals of pop mythology. Was it obscene? A Government committee spent some months playing *Louie Louie* every which way in an attempt to find out, and their findings were hardly reassuring to a nation already reeling from an onslaught of obnoxious, foul-mouthed popsters. No way could a ban be enacted, however. The song was just too popular, and its lyrics so obscure, that to try and stem the tide would be a waste of time and effort. *Louie Louie* lives on in radio mythology, long after the Kingsmen themselves have been forgotten.

The Kingsmen were followed out of Portland by Paul Revere And The Raiders, a band who enjoyed something approaching national acclaim when they hit with the jokey *Like, Long Hair*. They, too, had had their eye on *Louie Louie*, and expressed their displeasure at having been beaten to the punch with a quite withering response, *Louie Louie Go Home*. The nascent David Bowie, feeling the same way about the song's absorption into every British R&B band's repertoire, later borrowed it for his first ever B-side.

Although it was to take future historians to piece together some kind of cohesive movement from the hoard of garage bands which appeared in the wake of the Kingsmen, there was at least some unity to the pack: firstly in the sound — when the Beatles and The Beach Boys grew too sophisticated to copy, the infinitely less painstaking Byrds and Yardbirds stepped into the breach; and secondly in the powers who were to make the greatest impact on the marketing side of things. Because it was the marketing which would ultimately determine whether something was going to be a pop record . . . or a Pop Phenomenon. And getting that right was a talent in itself.

~ 1 ~
Tommy Facenda

1959: *High School USA*

Back around the turn of the 1950's, the wise old owls of Tin Pan Alley hit upon the notion of marketing High School as a viable teenage commodity. Rock and Roll really did seem to be over — death (Buddy Holly, Eddie Cochran), imprisonment (Chuck Berry), religion (Little Richard) and the draft (Elvis Presley) had seen to that. Nothing had come along to replace them, either, and the kids had no alternative but to return to the healthy, traditional values which had occupied their time in the years before the Revolution.

High School epitomized those values. It was also a pretext which Tin Pan Alley understood, a succession of spot-free adolescents with neat hair and sunny smiles, football hunks and cheerleading cuties whose (almost traditional) lack of singing ability was either ignored or else totally buried beneath layers of candy-sweet backing vocals and string sections.

It was portrayed as Pop Music, but it was more than that, it was a way of life. Everybody went to school, everybody loved their school — even the bad kids from the wrong side of the tracks, who spent their schooldays dodging class and riding motorcycles around the parking lot, even they would turn out to cheer the football team on, or dig out the bike chains when it was time for a rumble. That was the market at which High School was targeted, and it milked that love for all it was worth.

In 1959, a 20 year old Norfolk, Virginia session vocalist named Tommy "Bubba" Facenda recorded a song called *High School USA (Virginia)*, and set a standard, both musical and numerical, which has still to be eclipsed. Scholastic devotion simply didn't come deeper than this.

A former back up singer with Gene Vincent, Facenda had been discovered by starmaker Frank Guida, and released his first, flop, single in 1958. A couple more followed, but Guida knew it was only a matter of time before Facenda hit big — and he had just the song to make that happen — *High School USA (Virginia)*. Released by the tiny Legrand label, of course the record became a regional Virginia hit. But that was all it could ever hope to be, unless . . .

With the phone ringing off the hook with calls for *(Virginia)* to be followed by Arkansas, New York, Colorado, Alabama, California, wherever, Guida linked with Atlantic Records and set the ball in motion. The praises expressed in *High School USA (Virginia)* were so universal, so all pervading, that the song appealed across the board. The solution — 50 states in the union, 50 versions of the song.

In the end, Facenda recorded the song a mere 28 more times, but still each different version introduced a new region to the song's refrain: "High School USA (Boston)," "High School USA (Buffalo")," "High School USA (Chicago)" on and on to Washington DC. Had the records' sales justified it, the list could have gone on even further, but when the record stalled at No. 28, so did Facenda's geography . . . and so did his career. A mild mannered follow up, *Little Baby*, went nowhere, and Facenda eventually left the music business for a career as a fireman.

Neither did anybody seriously attempt repeating Facenda's experiment, but they didn't really need to. *High School (USA)* had proven both the strengths, and the resilience of a market which most pop entrepreneurs believed was simply there for the taking. And though nobody would be making the same mistakes again, they would be pursuing the same goals.

Discography:
Singles
  ○ *High School USA (Virginia)* / *Give me Another Chance* (Legrand 101, 1959)
  ○ *High School USA (Virginia)* / *Plea Of Love* (Atlantic 51, 1959)
  ○ *High School USA (NYC)* / *Plea Of Love* (Atlantic 52, 1959)
  ○ *High School USA (NC)* / *Plea Of Love* (Atlantic 53, 1959)
  ○ *High School USA (SC)* / *Plea Of Love* (Atlantic 54, 1959)
  ○ *High School USA (DC)* / *Plea Of Love* (Atlantic 55, 1959)
  ○ *High School USA (Philadelphia)* / *Plea Of Love* (Atlantic 56, 1959)
  ○ *High School USA (Detroit)* / *Plea Of Love* (Atlantic 57, 1959)
  ○ *High School USA (Pittsburgh)* / *Plea Of Love* (Atlantic 58, 1959)
  ○ *High School USA (Minn & St Paul)* / *Plea Of Love* (Atlantic 59, 1959)
  ○ *High School USA (FL)* / *Plea Of Love* (Atlantic 60, 1959)
  ○ *High School USA (Newark)* / *Plea Of Love* (Atlantic 61, 1959)
  ○ *High School USA (Boston)* / *Plea Of Love* (Atlantic 62, 1959)
  ○ *High School USA (Cleveland)* / *Plea Of Love* (Atlantic 63, 1959)
  ○ *High School USA (Buffalo)* / *Plea Of Love* (Atlantic 64, 1959)
  ○ *High School USA (Hartford)* / *Plea Of Love* (Atlantic 65, 1959)
  ○ *High School USA (Nashville)* / *Plea Of Love* (Atlantic 66, 1959)
  ○ *High School USA (Indianapolis)* / *Plea Of Love* (Atlantic 67, 1959)
  ○ *High School USA (Chicago)* / *Plea Of Love* (Atlantic 68, 1959)
  ○ *High School USA (New Orleans)* / *Plea Of Love* (Atlantic 69, 1959)
  ○ *High School USA (St Louis / Kansas City)* / *Plea Of Love* (Atlantic 70, 1959)
  ○ *High School USA (GA / AL)* / *Plea Of Love* (Atlantic 71, 1959)
  ○ *High School USA (Cincinatti)* / *Plea Of Love* (Atlantic 72, 1959)
  ○ *High School USA (Memphis)* / *Plea Of Love* (Atlantic 73, 1959)
  ○ *High School USA (LA)* / *Plea Of Love* (Atlantic 74, 1959)

- High School USA (San Francisco) / Plea Of Love (Atlantic 75, 1959)
- High School USA (TX) / Plea Of Love (Atlantic 76, 1959)
- High School USA (Seattle / Portland) / Plea Of Love (Atlantic 77, 1959)
- High School USA (OK) / Plea Of Love (Atlantic 78, 1959)

~ 2 ~
Cliff Richard

1963: *Summer Holiday*

His American profile flickers somewhere around a handful of hits which oldies radio barely remembers, and an iconic cult status whose very heartbeat pounds the words "Britain's best kept secret." In a career which has now spanned more than 42 years and over 100 hit singles, Cliff Richard remains as capable of topping the British charts today (his *Millennium Prayer* was No. 1 through November / December 1999) as he was way back when — *Travellin' Light* was his first chart topper, exactly 40 years before.

In between times, he withstood every new fashion, fad and flavor that the music industry could throw at him. From Beatlemania to grunge, glam, punk and techno, all bared their teeth in his direction, uttered a few derogatory comments about whatever they considered he represented (usually along the lines of middle-of-the-road Bible-bashing goody-two-shoes pap machines), and truly gave him their best shot. Cliff took them on the chin, then scored another hit. And where are Beatlemania, grunge, glam, punk and techno today?

Even today, the opening strains of Cliff's first single, *Move It*, ring with an almost apocalyptic self-assurance, the knowledge that without them, there would have been no Beatles, no Stones, no Sex Pistols, no Oasis, and if that wasn't immediately apparent when he first cut the song, he never showed it. Insistent beyond his years, confident beyond his then-apparent abilities, all spiffed out in his pink suit and sideburns, Cliff took the hopes and ambitions of an entire generation — his own — and turned them upside down. Of course the girls screamed at him ... you would, too, if he'd shown you what was possible.

Similarly, his first six albums, released in the UK between 1959-62 (but still unavailable in America), represent possibly THE most solid body of work of any individual (as in solo) performer in rock history, tracing Cliff's career as he ventured from rock demon to a more considered, ballad-tinged Christian.

Of course he was a child of his times — custom-built hits notwithstanding, Cliff's early repertoire essentially comprised the staples of every aspiring Rock and Roll band of the era: a bit of Buddy, a jot of Jerry Lee and, of course, a piece of Presley. On vinyl and in concert Cliff liked nothing more than to tangle with the King and *Kid Creole, Heartbreak Hotel, Jailhouse Rock, One Night, Lawdy Miss Clawdy, Blue Moon* — Cliff Richard may have been the greatest Rock and Roll artist Britain produced, but Elvis was still the yardstick, and the yardstick had some great songs.

Sung them pretty well, too, "since my baby left me . . ." Yeah, but Cliff sang them pretty well also. "I've found a new place to dwell . . ." Nine out of then housewives would be able to tell them apart, but down at the end of lonely street, wasn't there just a hint more raw emotion in the way Cliff signs the registry?

CLIFF, the then-wild young iconoclast's debut album, was recorded live at Abbey Road, in front of an invited (and very vocal) audience of fans, and its 16 tracks probably say more for the naive exuberance of early British Rock and Roll than any number of learned theses and scholarly tomes. With Cliff himself backed, as he would be for the next ten years, by the Shadows (at a time when they were still called the Drifters), CLIFF is a magnificent portrait of the team's capabilities — the band themselves throw three instrumentals into the brew, including a devastating *Be Bop A Lula*, with guitarist Hank Marvin already perfecting the licks and lines which would soon establish him as the role model for every British guitarist of the next five years.

Cliff, however, remains the star of the show, and tracing his own progress through the albums which followed, one can only marvel at the ease with which he fit into whatever mold the material demanded. Still rocking on 1959's CLIFF SINGS, slowing down (and tailored-suiting up) for ME AND MY SHADOWS (1960) and LISTEN TO CLIFF (1961), by the time he released 21 TODAY, just in time for his own 21st birthday in 1961, he was arguably the most accomplished, and certainly the most adventurous, vocalist to emerge from the entire Rock and Roll boom, British or American. And from a exhaustingly maniacal *20 Flight Rock*, through to a dementedly infectious *Beat Out Dat Rhythm On A Drum*, there wasn't a soul could touch him for versatility.

Within a year of 21 TODAY, of course, the arrival of the Beatles had already consigned him to Boring Old Fartdom, and the cue for a swift slide into forgotten oblivion. Yet he adapted to that as well — adapted and survived. 32 MINUTES . . ., Cliff's last album before Brian Epstein rewrote the rule book, sets its boundaries with covers of *Blueberry Hill* and the Rodgers / Hart show tune *Falling In Love With Love*; brings a new voice to *Spanish Harlem* just months after Ben E. King's original hit version, and opens with one of his liveliest 45's of the era, the Rock and Rolling *It'll Be Me*. The generation gap may have built a bridge right over him, but Cliff wasn't slowing down for anyone.

"[When] the Beatles and the Stones and so on came through, psychologically there was a bit of pressure [on us] because the media forgot about the rest of us," Cliff recalled. "It was only when a year had gone by that we started to say, 'wait a minute, why are we scared?' We were still on tour, we were still in the Top 5 regularly, what more could we ask for? So the fear kind of left and we realized we were able to compete from our little corner and that's just what we did. We just forgot about the rest of them, carried on, and they've all come and gone in the thousands and I'm still going."

Of course, it can be argued that Rock and Roll in the years before the Beatles was a very different beast to "rock" in the years thereafter. When Cliff's career started, a British performer was expected to spend a few years on the pop chart, then gravitate to weightier concerns — stage shows, movies, family entertainment. There was no room for the weighty pretensions of later "artistes" and no need for them either. Let politicians worry about the state of the world, let sociologists bemoan the nightmares of a generation, "pop" was short for popular and there was enough bad news in the papers. Entertainers were meant to make you smile and Cliff, his career guided and advised by some of the noblest names in the entertainment industry, was happy to follow suit. Within reason.

At the time of his breakthrough, in 1958, Cliff was (in the parlance of the day), "the boy who rocked the world." America had already had its Rock and Rolling day — Elvis was off in the army, Haley's comet was chasing its tail, and Little Richard was of little account. Cliff, on the other hand, was still coming down from his first hit single when he was co-opted for his first film, SERIOUS CHARGE, and the gritty realism of the movie's theme, a wild youth's insistence that he was indecently assaulted by the local vicar, summed up Cliff's box office appeal. It was also a lot more brutal than anything Elvis came up with on screen.

Cliff was rough, Cliff was tough, and the songs he performed on the soundtrack, *No Turning Back* and *Mad About You*, adhered perfectly to that image. So did a third number, the rollicking *Living Doll*, but Cliff would soon change that. Although the singer loved the song, he disliked its up tempo rock arrangement, and by the time it became his first No. 1, *Living Doll* had been transformed into his first major ballad, and the template around which much of his subsequent career was designed.

Certainly it's no surprise that many of Cliff's biggest hits over the next five years should also be ballads, nor that the musical highlights of his next three movies would supply many of the most memorable examples. *A Voice In The Wilderness* and the surprisingly moving *The Shrine On The Second Floor* (from EXPRESSO BONGO, 1959); *When The Girl In Your Arms* (THE YOUNG ONES, 1961); *The Next Time* and the freakishly prophetic *Bachelor Boy* (SUMMER HOLIDAY, 1962) are no strangers to a thousand Best Of Cliff collections, and the only injustice is that their radiance often blinded listeners to some equally deserving material.

Cliff remained at his unquestioned peak until 1965, when *The Minute You're Gone* gave him his eighth No. 1 in six years, but his last for another three. He continued to tour, of course, but it was indeed within the increasingly "adult" confines which had been his destiny at the start. Christmas, 1964, saw him appearing at the London Palladium in a musical production of ALADDIN AND HIS WONDERFUL LAMP. The following year, he came within a whisker of recording an entire album of songs from old Walt Disney movies. 1966 included a starring role in a ghastly version of CINDERELLA. Like the audience which had followed him since *Move It*, Cliff was suddenly into his early-mid 20's, an adult in the understanding of the day, and content to leave the pop to the kids.

"By the mid-1960's, the bands which had just broken through brought in a whole new breed of musician. People like myself and the Shadows were the tail end of vaudeville — I remember shows when we had stilt walkers and jugglers supporting us. Everything was very, very pukka, very acceptable, very clean."

"Then the Beatles and the Stones and everyone came along and you suddenly discovered your favorite pop stars took drugs and lived in caves in India with Maharishis and threw television sets full of porridge out of hotel windows, and it changed everything. Anybody would look good compared with that. I got my 'goody two shoes' image through being completely normal, which goes to show how perverse our society is, that what is seen as wholesome has an alienating effect on some people."

This sense of unnatural wholesomeness, of course, was only exacerbated by Cliff's very public conversion to Christianity at a Billy Graham rally in London in 1966. Rumors that he was quitting music to pursue this new life were prevalent for a time, and there was a point when he truly wondered how he could reconcile his career with his religion. "All my friends who were Christians were teaching religion in schools, working for charitable organizations, and I thought 'oh dear, there's them being proper Christians and here's me rocking it up and having a great time.' So I thought I'd get out."

He wrapped up his fan club, tidied up his business affairs, stopped taking further live and recording engagements. His retirement was already solid in his mind when suddenly, everything changed. His record label, Columbia, offered him the opportunity to record a gospel album (1967's GOOD NEWS, the first of five gospel albums he cut over the next 13 years.) The BBC asked him to host a six show television series on his faith, and the media couldn't get enough of the Holy Rock and Roller. "And I thought, 'hang on, I can be a Christian in my business. I can make use of my business.' So I stayed."

In 1968, Cliff scored that aforementioned first No. 1 hit in three years when *Congratulations*, Britain's entry for that year's Eurovision Song Contest, went all the way at home, even as it was pipped at the post in the Contest itself. Neither would his luck change with a second bite at the Eurovision cherry in 1973 — *Power To All Our Friends*, too, finished second although again there was a monster home hit to dull the pain. *Power To All Our Friends* made it to No. 4, a lowly rank according to past performances, but at this point in time, a welcome affirmation that he was still a viable force on the music scene.

Congratulations was followed by a period of almost nightmarish under-achievement. Single after single seemed incapable of climbing even into the Top 10. The man who had spent the past decade effortlessly plucking hit material from whichever source offered it, suddenly seemed hopelessly out of touch with the tastes of even a tiny portion of his fan base. He was lost, his repertoire was stale, his image was atrocious. But his determination was undiminished. In 1972, Cliff broke with Norrie Paramour, his producer and musical mentor since *Move It*. He linked with the younger Dave MacKay and two years later, 31ST OF FEBRUARY STREET became his first new album in almost a decade to actually sound and feel like an album, as opposed to a simple mish mash of songs from a string of disconnected sessions.

It was his next album, however, which would spell Cliff's rebirth. I'M NEARLY FAMOUS was previewed by the utterly spellbinding *Miss You Nights* in January, 1976. The oddly-disco tinged *I Can't Ask For Anything More than You* followed. And then came *Devil Woman*, an absolute masterpiece which made No. 9 in Britain and an unprecedented No. 6 in America.

Better was to come. Though neither was a classic, the albums EVERY FACE TELLS A STORY and GREEN LIGHT both returned Cliff to his old Rock and Roll throne, albeit from a decidedly mature point of view — and rightly, sensibly so. At the height of punk, it seemed somehow bizarre to catch a nearly 40-year-old whooping it up on Top Of The Pops, but it was reassuring as well, a reminder that even with the entire world in flames, some things had come through the furnace unscathed. Five years earlier, Cliff would have crumbled with the rest of them.

1980's ROCK AND ROLL JUVENILE was the true heir to I'M NEARLY FAMOUS, from the worldwide No. 1 *We Don't Talk Anymore*, through the playful *Hotshot* and onto the song which not only became Cliff's first hit of the decade, but also proved that he was going to have no problem whatsoever dealing with it. *Carrie*, written by the then-fashionable BA Robertson, was simply superlative — it was certainly one of Cliff's best performances in years and, had he followed its lead for a little longer, the enormous strides he'd made in the past five years would doubtless have continued.

Instead, he consolidated, not only his position, but also his career — 1983's SILVER album, marking his 25th year of recording, saw him delightedly plundering his back catalog for a good natured selection of remakes and rewrites. Hits-heavy live albums and concert spectaculars became increasingly regular occurrences. He moved deeper into theatrical work and music — a starring role in Dave Clarke's TIME musical (he was replaced by David Cassidy at the end of his contracted year's run), soundtrack work for PHANTOM OF THE OPERA and HUNTING OF THE SNARK, and regular Christmas singles. 1994 even saw him launch his own musical, a well-received adaptation of WUTHERING HEIGHTS, HEATHCLIFF.

And the hits kept coming. In 1970, *Goodbye Sam, Hello Samantha* became his 50th single. In 1989, he celebrated his 100th, *The Best Of Me*. And 1999 brought the aforementioned *Millennium Prayer*, a majestic blending of the Lord's Prayer and *Auld lang Syne* which, incredibly, his record company of the past 42 years refused to release. Cliff quit the label, gave the song to his manager's newly formed indie, and spent the next five weeks at No. 1. He later admitted that as much as any other triumph in his career, from *Move It* to *Miss You Nights* to becoming a Knight (he was made Sir Cliff in October, 1995), that was one triumph he would never forget.

Discography:
Singles
  ○ *Lucky Lips / Next Time* (Epic 9597, 1963)
  ○ *It's All In The Game / I'm Looking Out The Window* (Epic 9633, 1963)
  ○ *I'm The Lonely One / I Only Have Eyes For You* (Epic 9670, 1964)
  ○ *Bachelor Boy / True, True Lovin'* (Epic 9691, 1964)
  ○ *I Don't Wanna Love You / Look In My Eyes Maria* (Epic 9737, 1964)
  ○ *Again / The Minute You're Gone* (Epic 9757, 1965)
  ○ *I Could Easily Fall (In Love With You) / On My Word* (Epic 9810, 1965)
  ○ *The Twelfth Of Never / Paradise Lost* (Epic 9839, 1965)
  ○ *Wind Me Up (And Let Me Go) / Eye Of A Needle* (Epic 9866, 1965)
  ○ *Blue Turns To Grey / I'll Walk Alone* (Epic 10018, 1966)
  ○ *Visions / Quando, Quando, Quando* (Epic 10070, 1966)
  ○ *Time Drags By / The La La La Song* (Epic 10101, 1966)
  ○ *It's All Over / Heartbeat* (Epic 10178, 1967)
  ○ *All My Love / Our Story Book* (Uni 55061, 1968)
  ○ *Congratulations / High 'N' Dry* (Uni 55069, 1968)

- *The Day I Met Marie / Sweet Little Jesus Boy* (Uni 55145, 1969)
- *Throw Down A Line / Reflections* (Warner Bros. 7344, 1969)
- *Goodbye Sam, Hello Samantha / You Never Can Tell* (Monument 1211, 1970)
- *I Ain't Got Time Anymore / Morning Comes Too Soon* (Monument 1229, 1970)
- *Living In Harmony / Jesus* (Sire 703, 1973)
- *Power To All Our Friends / Come Back Billie Joe* (Sire 707, 1973)
- *Miss You Nights / Love Enough* (Rocket 40531, 1976)
- *Devil Woman / Love On (Shine On)* (Rocket 40574, 1976)
- *Junior Cowboy / I Can't Ask For Anymore Than You* (Rocket 40652, 1976)
- *Don't Turn The Light Out / Nothing Left For Me To Say* (Rocket 40724, 1977)
- *You've Got Me Wondering / Try A Smile* (Rocket 40771, 1977)
- *Green Light / Needing A Friend* (Rocket RB-11463, 1979)
- *We Don't Talk Anymore / Count Me Out* (EMI America 8025, 1979)
- *Carrie / Language Of Love* (EMI America 8035, 1980)
- *Dreaming / Dynamite* (EMI America 8057, 1980)
- *A Little In Love / Everyman* (EMI America 8068, 1980)
- *Give A Little Bit More / Keep Lookin'* (EMI America 8076, 1981)
- *Wired For Sound / Hold On* (EMI America 8095, 1981)
- *Daddy's Home / Summer Rain* (EMI America 8103, 1982)
- *The Only Way Out / Be In My Heart* (EMI America 8135, 1982)
- *Little Town / Be In My Heart* (EMI America 8149, 1982)
- *Never Say Die (Give A Little Bit More) / Front Page* (EMI America 8180, 1983)
- *Donna / Ocean Deep* (EMI America 8193, 1984)
- *All I Ask Of You / Phantom Of The Opera Overture, Act 2* (Polydor 885 336-7, 1987)
- *My Pretty One / Love Ya* (Striped Horse 7008, 1988)
- *Some People / Love Ya* (Striped Horse 7011, 1988)

Albums
- SUMMER HOLIDAY (Epic 24063, 1963)
- IT'S ALL IN THE GAME (Epic 24089, 1964)
- SWINGERS PARADISE (Epic 26145, 1964)
- CLIFF RICHARD IN SPAIN (Epic 24115, 1965)
- GOOD NEWS (Word 8507, 1967)
- TWO A PENNY (Uni 1086, 1968)
- HIS LAND (Light 5532, 1970)
- I'M NEARLY FAMOUS (Rocket 2210, 1976)
- EVERY FACE TELLS A STORY (Rocket 2268, 1977)
- GREEN LIGHT (Rocket 2958, 1978)
- WE DON'T TALK ANYMORE (EMI America 17018, 1979)
- I'M NO HERO (EMI America 17039, 1980)
- WIRED FOR SOUND (EMI America 17059, 1981)
- NOW YOU SEE ME, NOW YOU DON'T (EMI America 17081, 1982)
- GIVE A LITTLE BIT MORE (EMI America 17105, 1983)
- WALKING IN THE LIGHT (Word 8306, 1985)

~ 3 ~
Herman's Hermits

1965: *Mrs. Brown You've Got A Lovely Daughter*

Through the first heady days of American Beatlemania, any number of starry-eyed young hopefuls threatened — at least in the eyes of the teenaged press — to dislodge the Moptops from their lofty nook. The Dave Clark Five, for a time, inspired fan worship at least as fanatical as the Fabs, but only for a time. The Rolling Stones, too, enjoyed a moment in the teenybop sun, before the group's studied pose of anti-social grimness sent the dreamboat to the bottom. Freddy And The Dreamers, Gerry And The Pacemakers, the Hollies, they all had a stab and then stumbled. But one group not only looked capable of assuming the Beatles' mantel, for a short while they might even have done so. It was Herman's Hermits, and for anyone under ten years old, Herman made the Beatles look like grandfathers.

A five piece hailing from the northern English city of Manchester, just down the road from the Beatles' Liverpool hometown, Herman's Hermits were purveyors of a bubbling confection which, frankly, made the Beatles sound obtuse.

In the beginning, of course, the band was nothing like that. It took the arrival in their ranks of singer Peter Noone, wide-smiled angelic teen actor and soap star, to transform the Heartbeats from hardworking Mancunian club band to superstars in waiting. But once the transformation had been effected, there was no looking back.

Painfully enthusiastic, blisteringly innocent, Noone resembled nothing so much as the cartoon character Sherman from TV's "Rocky And Bullwinkle" series . . . or so Heartbeats' bassist Karl Green reckoned, when he renamed the singer Herman. The band became the Hermits shortly after, and in early 1964, they were "discovered" on stage in nearby Bolton by would-be manager/record producer Micky Most.

The Hermits — Derek Leckenby, Keith Hopwood, Karl Green and Barry Whitham — interested Most, but it was Herman who fascinated him. "His manager sent me a postcard of [Peter] standing opposite Picadilly Station in Manchester, where there's a sort of fountain. I looked at this group of young sort of tear-aways, and Peter, or Herman, stood out as being like a young John F. Kennedy, and that was what attracted me, because I thought he had a face for America."

It was an astute observation. The Beatles had yet to crack America at that time — they had yet to even appear there, as a string of disinterested minor labels released a handful of their records to little or no public response. In Britain, however, the Beatles were unleashing a tidal wave of teenybop hunger, and Most saw Herman having the same effect. All he had to do was get across the ocean ahead of the Fabs.

Of course he didn't, but the dream remained intact. Few of the acts which followed in the Beatles' wake, after all, had been capable, or even deserving, of making more than a token try for their share of the largess. But Most knew from the start that if he could just pair Herman's beguiling looks with a song which matched his magic, the results would be spectacular.

I'm Into Something Good was just such a song. A cover of Earl-Jean of the Cookies' recent US hit, written by the nigh-on fail-safe duo of Goffin / King, the song was a stupendous statement of youthful intent and vigor. Certainly it lost little time in galloping up both the UK and US charts, and while a follow-up from the same song writing stable, *Show Me Girl*, did little (proving, once again, how difficult follow-up hits were in the world of teenbeat poppery), by early 1965, both *Silhouettes* and a cover of Sam Cooke's *Wonderful World* had re-established Herman's Hermits as a force in the land.

Can't You Hear My Heartbeat, the Hermits' second American splash, coincided with a cameo in one of the movie hits of the year, Connie Francis' WHERE THE BOYS MEET THE GIRLS, and rapidly, Most's vision of the Hermits as an American phenomenon began to pay off. Indeed, the group's American profile swiftly shot away at a total tangent to its British counterpart — at home, the Hermits were a lightweight pop group churning out a string of likable, but largely harmless hits. In America, they were mega, with a career which the British fans simply would not have recognized.

What would become Herman's Hermits' signature hit, *Mrs. Brown, You've Got A Lovely Daughter*, was not even released a single in the UK, yet it topped the American chart with effortless ease . . . effortless as Micky Most claims he doesn't even remember recording what he subsequently described as, "probably the worst record ever made, or at least the worst one that I've been associated with."

He told the BBC's Record Producers series, "we got a phone call from MGM in America saying they needed an album by Thursday, and I got the lads down from wherever they were, and we had to decide what we'd record. I asked them what they were doing on stage at the time and they muttered something about 'Mrs. Brown,' so I said let's do it. We sent it out to America and three weeks later we got a phone call saying they wanted to put it out as a single."

Mrs. Brown, You've Got A Lovely Daughter, a chirpy blend of bubblegum pop and music hall quirkiness, went on to become one of the fastest selling singles of the year — according to Most, it sold over three-quarters of a million copies in one day. Indeed, 1965 saw Herman's Hermits release half-a-dozen million selling singles, plus a GREATEST HITS collection which was no less successful. And rockist accusations that they were simply churning out pap for the masses didn't phase them in the slightest. "No-one was taking their music seriously," Most reflected. "They were just fun on the radio, up, sunshine music, and that way you could be flippant and do it lightheartedly."

Just A Little Bit Better, You Won't Be Leaving, A Must To Avoid and *East West*, and the Graham Gouldman classic *No Milk Today* kept the group's success boiling throughout 1966, while a couple of movies, HOLD ON and the inevitable MRS. BROWN, YOU'VE GOT A LOVELY DAUGHTER ensured that the group's sheer popularity knew no bounds. Kids loved them, parents loved them, grandparents loved them. At a time when other pop idols were growing beards and getting attitudes, Herman remained the same lovable grinning boy next door he always had been, and as one wave of fans grew too old for the Hermits' super fluff, their younger siblings rose up to take their place.

"They were incredibly popular," Most mused. "I can remember going to places in America where they'd have a Herman's Hermits day, and everybody would have a public holiday, and Pete was made Governor of the town or given Freedom of the State or whatever. It was amazing." And it was unstoppable. While other bands of the Hermits' era, the Beatles, the Stones, the Kinks, whoever, drifted into psychedelia and gave up making singles for the kiddies, the Hermits remained defiantly loyal to the genre, and opened 1967 in precisely the same way they'd seen out 1966, with the multi million selling *There's A Kind Of Hush (All Over The World)*. The following year, *Something Is Happening* maintained the band's proud record of one unforgettable monster smash every 12 months, and in 1969, *My Sentimental Friend* did the same.

A noticeable slackening in the hysteria which awaited every new Hermits single was appreciable, though, and a falling away of the riotous pandemonium which greeted every live performance was evident as well. When the Hermits toured America in the summer of 1967, the screams of the audience were loud enough to drown even the Who, the oddly chosen support act for the outing. A year later, however, the screams had subsided, and though the band's records remained as irresistible as ever — a curiously innocent cover of Ray Davies' archly knowing *Dandy*, the maddening *Sunshine Girl*, Donovan's *Museum* — it became apparent that their music alone would never sustain the band's career. So they did the only sensible thing they could do — and broke up.

Noone, having pushed his name to the fore on the band's late 1970 *Lady Barbara* single, now went solo, and scored an immediate hit with a handsomely clunky version of the then-unknown David Bowie's *Oh, You Pretty Things*; the Hermits, with new vocalist Peter Cowap, moved deliberately into the golden oldies circuit, after a string of 45's cut with the 10cc crew in Manchester went nowhere. And while there was a tremendous Herman's Hermits reunion show at Madison Square Garden in 1973, it was clear that past glories could never be recaptured. So they never even tried.

Discography:

Singles

- *I'm Into Something Good / Your Hand In Mine* (MGM 13280, 1964)
- *Can't You Hear My Heartbeat / I Know Why* (MGM 13310, 1965)
- *Silhouettes / Walkin' With My Angel* (MGM 13332, 1965)
- *Mrs Brown, You've Got A Lovely Daughter / I Gotta Dream On* (MGM 13341, 1965)
- *Wonderful World / Travelin' Light* (MGM 13354, 1965)
- *I'm 'enery The Eighth I Am / End Of The World* (MGM 13367, 1965)
- *Just A Little Bit Better / Sea Cruise* (MGM 13398, 1965)
- *A Must To Avoid / Man With The Cigar* (MGM 13437, 1965)
- *Listen People / Got A Feeling* (MGM 13462, 1966)
- *Leaning On The Lamp Post / Hold On* (MGM 13500, 1966)
- *This Door Swings Both Ways / For Love* (MGM 13548, 1966)
- *Dandy / My Reservation's Been Confirmed* (MGM 13603, 1966)
- *East West / What Is Wrong, What Is Right* (MGM 13639, 1966)
- *There's A Kind Of Hush / No Milk Today* (MGM 13681, 1967)
- *Don't Go Out In The Rain / Moonshine Men* (MGM 13761, 1967)
- *Museum / Moonshine Men* (MGM 13787, 1967)
- *I Can Take Or Leave Your Loving / Marcel's* (MGM 13885, 1968)
- *Sleepy Joe / Just On Girl* (MGM 13934, 1968)
- *Sunshine Girl / Nobody Needs To Know* (MGM 13973, 1968)
- *The Most Beautiful Thing In My Life / Ooh She's Done It Again* (MGM 13994, 1968)
- *Something's Happening / Little Miss Sorrow* (MGM 14035, 1968)
- *My Sentimental Friend / My Lady* (MGM 14060, 1969)
- *Here Comes The Star / It's Alright Now* (MGM 14100, 1969)

Albums

- INTRODUCING (MGM 4282, 1965)
- ON TOUR (MGM 4296, 1965)
- HERMAN'S HERMITS (MGM 4382, 1965)
- THE BEST OF (MGM 4315, 1965)
- WHERE THE BOYS MEET THE GIRLS (MGM 4334, 1965)
- HOLD ON (MGM 4342, 1966)
- BOTH SIDES OF (MGM 4386, 1966)
- THE BEST OF VOLUME TWO (MGM 4416, 1966)
- THERE'S A KIND OF HUSH (MGM 4438, 1967)
- BLAZE (MGM 4478, 1967)
- THE BEST OF VOLUME THREE (MGM 4505, 1968)
- MRS BROWN YOU'VE GOT A LOVELY DAUGHTER (MGM 4548, 1968)

~ 4 ~
The Walker Brothers

1966: *The Sun Ain't Gonna Shine*

The moment they landed in London, it was apparent that they had something. The Walker Brothers were not brothers: they weren't even named Walker. But they had Beatle haircuts and California tans, and when Scott Engel opened his mouth to sing, all human heartache was there on display.

In truth, there wasn't much original about the Walker Brothers. Back home in America (which never really took to them, even after they became stars in Britain), the three had worked together with no more success than attended any number of other good looking boys attempting to cut a pop career in the heart of Hollywood. Even after stardom struck, their best records were all essentially continuations of Phil Spector's recent Righteous Brothers successes, while their choice of material, the odd Dylan cover included, was little different to the kind of fare any number of middle-of-the-roady pop vocalists were serving up right then.

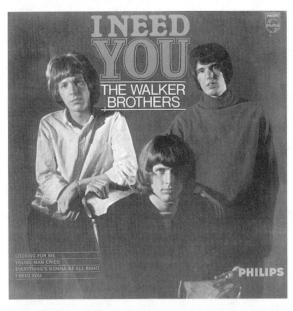

The difference was front man Scott Walker. He didn't sing, he opened his mouth and let a dolorous dollop of pain fall out instead. *Love Her*, the Walkers' first British hit, and *Make It Easy On Yourself* and *The Sun Ain't Gonna Shine Anymore*, both UK number ones, are still affecting today, Wagnerian epics of desertion and doom, while *My Ship Is Coming In*, a No. 2, is delivered with such deathly irony that you know it isn't really. It's foundering on the rocks somewhere, taking in water and waiting for the end. Just like Scott himself. And though the singer waited for his solo career to begin before he unleashed his love for Jacques Brel on a bewildered world, the roots of that romance were already plain to see. Of course the sun ain't gonna shine anymore. You keep your curtains closed all day.

As the Walker Brothers' best-known recordings on either side of the Atlantic, *Easy*, *Sun* and *Ship* naturally lie at the heart of the trio's posthumous reputation. Where it goes from there, though, is another thing entirely, as Walker delved deep into a world of (chiefly European) art as pain to unleash such doom-laden gems as *In My Room*, or else took standard soul inflected chest baring ballads as *Stay With Me Baby*, and transformed them into suicide notes — which, of course, is how it almost all ended up, as Walker proved himself utterly unable to live the life of the merely reclusive icon which his fans demanded, and hankered instead for a hermitage.

His rumored suicide attempt did much to take the edge off the hysteria which haunted him; his solo career did the rest. A rendering of Jacques Brel's *Jackie*, Walker's biggest solo hit, was all but disowned by his own fan club, so outraged were they by the song's gratuitous references to a life of unbridled debauchery. And while just six months divided SCOTT I from the Walkers' IMAGES, in musical terms, the group could have come from a different age.

By the time of his fourth album, Walker's introspection was so deep that the record was released under his all-but unknown real name, Noel Engels, and the catchiest thing in sight was the hook which the sensitive listener hanged himself from. SCOTT 4 bombed completely, selling so few copies that it was deleted within nine months. Considering the three albums before it had all made Britain's Top Three, that was quite an achievement.

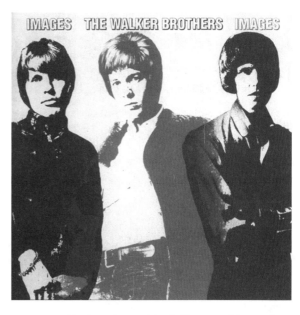

But Walker still wasn't satisfied. Having reinvented himself as a human Armageddon, he now stopped writing his own songs, gave up on Brel, embraced bad Country Music, then reformed the Walker Brothers for the cabaret circuit. From iconoclast to *Iko Iko* — not even David Bowie could move that fast! And when the wheels fell off that wagon, he started heading back again, digging himself into a suitably claustrophobic pit, then digging it even deeper.

He signed an eight album deal with Virgin Records in 1979, and didn't deliver his first disc until 1984. He was dropped shortly after. Twelve years later, he released a follow-up, TILT, then disappeared once again, knowing only that the record moved so far from the rock mainstream within which Walker has proved so retrospectively influential, that the Walker Brothers themselves weren't simply a lifetime away. They were now a few solar systems distant as well.

Discography:

Singles

- *Pretty Girls Everywhere / Doin' The Jerk* (Smash 1952, 1965)
- *Love Her / The Seventh Dawn* (Smash 1976, 1965)
- *Make It Easy On Yourself / But I Do* (Smash 2000, 1965)
- *My Ship Is Coming In / You're All Around Me* (Smash 2016, 1965)
- *The Sun Ain't Gonna Shine / After The Lights Go Out* (Smash 2032, 1966)
- *You Don't Have To Tell Me / My Love Is Growing* (Smash 2048, 1966)
- *Another Tear Falls / Saddest Night In The World* (Smash 2063, 1966)

Albums

- INTRODUCING (Smash 27076, 1966)
- THE SUN AIN'T GONNA SHINE (Smash 27082, 1966)

~ 5 ~
Tommy James And The Shondells

1966: *Hanky Panky*

In an ideal world, a true pop star would never have had to do something so mundane as sing. He or she would just stand around looking pretty and the media machine would take care of everything else. In an imperfect world, however, making records was a fact of life, and with it, the need to make the right song fit the right image.

With the exception of such pudgy (but genuinely talented) anomalies as Paul Anka and Neil Sedaka, the sound of High School emanated from the Hit Factories — indeed, Sedaka himself served his apprenticeship at one, Don Kirshner's Brill Building, and he wasn't alone. Of all the institutions that made American pop a pre-Beatles world beater (and of all those which the Beatles mercifully helped to extinguish), the Hit Factory was one of the most pernicious.

It was also, of course, a principle which both Tamla Motown and Kasenatz-Katz were later to employ, and according to English songwriter Graham Gouldman, who was to work at the latter during the late 1960's, the system ran along the simplest lines imaginable. "We were employed to write songs. Every morning we would clock in, go up to our offices, sit down at the piano and write. It was like any factory, only instead of little bits of cars, you'd make little bits of music." The criteria which bound their efforts were equally simple. Was a song easy to learn, easy to sing? Was it a hit? That was all that mattered.

By 1960 the heart of the industry was the Brill Building, at 1619 Broadway, New York. Don Kirshner and Al Nevins, the brains behind the operation, worked from an office across the road, and their demands were simple. You're writing for teenagers, so write about teenagers. Thus, their most inspired recruits were usually teenagers, or at least people young enough to remember what it was like to be one.

Carole King, Gerry Goffin, Bobby Darin, Barry Mann and Cynthia Weill, Neil Diamond, Gary Sherman, Neil Sedaka, Howie Greenfield, all filed into the Brill Building at 10 every morning, and as the writers settled into their roles, so styles and identities came to the fore. Between them, Goffin / King, Weill / Mann and Sedaka / Greenfield would be responsible for some fifty US hits over the next five years, and even after the Beatles had come to kill the contract songwriter dead, Goffin / King, at least, were to ride out the storm simply by beefing up their output and setting out to compete with the best of them.

Jeff Barry and Ellie Greenwich, another Brill coupling, followed Goffin / King into the new era, largely through their involvement with producers Phil Spector and Shadow Morton. British invaders Manfred Mann's first Stateside hit, *Doo Wah Diddy Diddy*, was one of three number ones the pair enjoyed during the crucial year of 1964, and they later came up with *River Deep, Mountain High*, *Chapel Of Love* and *Leader Of The Pack*. The truth of the matter, though, was that the Greenwich / Barry team was at its best when it was at its basest. Lyrically, *Da Doo Ron Ron*, *Baby I Love You* and *Doo Wah Diddy Diddy* meant next to nothing, but they sounded great. And in 1963, the pair came up with another song which fell directly into the same sub-literate category; the immortal *Hanky Panky*.

Tommy James And The Shondells, to whom the song was ceremoniously presented, might have been cut straight out of the High School mold, if only because they sounded just like Bobby Rydell and Co. had looked — clean cut, clean living and clean minded. Their appearance, on the other hand, left rather more to be desired. James himself was a rugged mass topped off with a mane of wild, wiry hair, and the rest of the band had all the appeal of a gang of Texan garage mechanics.

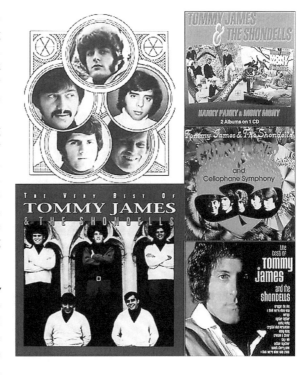

But with a song like *Hanky Panky*, none of that mattered. So what if James' vocals descended into a threatening growl? The song itself was genuine Pop, safe as milk and healthy as Herman. And while James never looked likely to challenge anyone in the Dreamboat of the Day stakes, in vinyl terms it quickly developed into a neck and neck race, the Hermits vs. the Shondells.

Not that it was plain sailing all the way. The first release of the Shondells' *Hanky Panky*, in 1963, went nowhere. Neither did a second, in 1965. But it was reissued again in the spring of '66, and this time there was no holding it back. *Hanky Panky* soared to No. 1, and just in case anybody thought it was a fluke, two more hits before the end of the year gave the Shondells a chart busting profile to die for. By March 1967, the competition was positively ferocious. On the one hand there was Herman hitting out with the double A-sided *No Milk Today / There's A Kind Of Hush*, on the other, Tommy James had *I Think We're Alone Now*, a song which is regarded today as the founding father of the entire Bubblegum scene.

In reality, that honor belongs to the Shondells' next big hit, one album and four minor successes later. *Mony Mony* not only boasted the naive musical exuberance of *I Think We're Alone Now*, but also encapsulated hints of so many other, earlier, pop hits — the joyous audience participation engendered by *The Name Game* and *The Clapping Song*, the call and response technique of *Iko Iko*, and to round it all off, a beat which was perfect for hopscotch.

However, while writer Ritchie Cordell was later to reap the credit for having created the Bubblegum song, the more important accolade of having created the Bubblegum sound was to pass him by. For while Cordell and the Shondells worked to perfect their own vision of pop at its tastiest, chewiest, bubbliest best, over at Colgems Records another familiar face had his own visions of how such a confection should sound.

Discography:
Singles
  ◦ *Hanky Panky / Thunderbolt* (Snap 102, 1963)
  ◦ *Hanky Panky / Thunderbolt* (Red Fox 110, 1965)
  ◦ *Hanky Panky / Thunderbolt* (Roulette 4686, 1966)
  ◦ *Say I Am (What I Am) / Lots Of Pretty Girls* (Roulette 4695, 1966)
  ◦ *It's Only Love / Ya Ya* (Roulette 4710, 1966)
  ◦ *I Think We're Alone Now / Gone Gone Gone* (Roulette 4720, 1967)
  ◦ *Mirage / Run Run Baby Run* (Roulette 4736, 1967)
  ◦ *I Like The Way / I Can't Take It No More* (Roulette 4756, 1967)
  ◦ *Gettin' Together / Real Girl* (Roulette 4762, 1967)
  ◦ *Out Of The Blue / Love's Closin' In On Me* (Roulette 4775, 1967)
  ◦ *Get Out Now / Wish It Were You* (Roulette 7000, 1968)
  ◦ *Mony Mony / 1,2,3 And I Fell* (Roulette 7008, 1968)
  ◦ *Somebody Cares / Do Unto Me* (Roulette 7016, 1968)
  ◦ *Do Something To Me / Gingerbread Man* (Roulette 7024, 1968)
  ◦ *Crimson & Clover / Some Kind Of Love* (Roulette 7028, 1968)
  ◦ *Sweet Cherry Wine / Breakaway* (Roulette 7039, 1969)
  ◦ *Crystal Blue Persuasion / I'm Alive* (Roulette 7050, 1969)
  ◦ *Ball Of Fire / Makin' Good Time* (Roulette 7060, 1969)
  ◦ *She / Loved One* (Roulette 7066, 1969)
  ◦ *Gotta Get Back To You / Red Rover* (Roulette 7071, 1970)
  ◦ *Come To Me / Talkin' & Signifin'* (Roulette 7076, 1970)

Albums
- HANKY PANKY (Roulette 25336, 1966)
- IT'S ONLY LOVE (Roulette 25344, 1966)
- I THINK WE'RE ALONE NOW (Roulette 25353, 1967)
- GETTIN' TOGETHER (Roulette 25357, 1967)
- SOMETHING SPECIAL! The Best Of (Roulette 25355, 1968)
- MONY MONY (Roulette 42012, 1968)
- CRIMSON & CLOVER (Roulette 42023, 1968)
- CELLOPHANE SYMPHONY (Roulette 42030, 1969)
- BEST OF (Roulette 42040, 1969)
- TRAVELLIN' (Roulette 42044, 1970)

~ 6 ~
The Monkees

1966: *I'm A Believer*

It is only with the benefit of hindsight that the Monkees ever came to be classified as Bubblegum, Pop, or any of those other indistinct terms used to describe music which an inordinate number of people like . . . or should like. For one thing, they pre-dated the Bubblegum boom itself by at least a year; by the time arch-gummeisters Kasenatz-Katz really hit their stride, the Monkees were virtually on their last legs.

Musically, too, the Monkees were too complex to fit perfectly into the Bubblegum slot. And yet the circumstances in which they were born, and the genres out of which they flowered, were identical to those which were to motivate the Bubblegum bang, while the bulk of their material was written by the same kind of people, under the same kind of conditions, as those who serviced Super K; Tommy Boyce and Bobby Hart, a latter-day Brill Building team. The only real difference was, the Monkees were real people. You could see them, you could write to them, you could fall in love with them.

The basic premise behind the Monkees was to capture the magic and mystique of Beatlemania through a medium whose potential had still to be fully exploited in terms of promoting new produce; television. With the exception, perhaps, of Elvis and the Beatles themselves, both of whom were to erupt only after the cathode tube beamed them into American society via the Ed Sullivan Show, the possibilities of the small screen had been totally ignored by the pop industry. Indeed, even those isolated examples which had hit were brought about more by accident than design. The Monkees changed all that.

"It was the demonstration of these two giant media complexes pooling their resources and promoting something together," says Monkees drummer Micky Dolenz. "It wouldn't have mattered if it had been the Monkees or a particular brand of soap. It was the first time in history that the two industries got in bed together to push a common product."

The Monkees' most obvious antecedent, of course, was the Beatles' film career, although the show's creators were later to claim that their idea actually predated both A HARD DAY'S NIGHT and HELP. But even before the band's line-up had been created, Raybert (the company set up by creators Rafelson and Schneider, and sponsored by the television wing of Columbia Pictures, Screen Gems) knew exactly the nature of the "insane boys" they were looking for when they ran the Daily Variety ad which invited "folk and rock musicians and singers" to come down for an interview. Thus, Harry Nilsson, Paul Williams, Danny Hutton, Steven Stills and, according to legend, Charles Manson, were all rejected, along with 428 other hopefuls, in favor of Micky Dolenz, Mike Nesmith, Peter Tork and Davy Jones.

Whether or not it was deliberate (and one tends to think it was), the four were natural for roles which, it was already being suggested around town, were designed as surrogate Beatles. Dolenz was the cute, cuddly one with the madcap sense of humor — Ringo; Nesmith the mature, intellectual one — Lennon, Tork the gawky guy every girl wanted to mother — McCartney, and little Davy Jones was there for everybody who still wanted a Beatle (Harrison) or at least a Herman. Like the head Hermit, Davy hailed from Manchester, England. He had the same little boy quality, a similar accent and he was, in fact, already contracted to Screen Gems, where Don Kirshner was toying with the idea of launching him as some kind of Peter Noone-like heart throb.

With Kirshner so close (he was President of the Music Division), it was obvious that Raybert would turn to him when it came to grafting music onto their creation. Within eighteen hours of their first call, Kirshner had already delivered a dozen backing tracks to the LA studio wherein the Monkees were ensconced. Ten more arrived a few days later — enough material for five episodes of the TV show, plus a debut album.

Kirshner had that in hand as well. He had negotiated for RCA Victor to distribute the Monkees' music via a specially created new label, Colgems. It cost RCA $10,000, and they set about recouping their money immediately, commissioning an unheard-of 76 advance men to wallpaper the United States with the seeds of Monkeemania. The Beatles were touring the country at the time, their last public outing before going serious, and their concerts proved ideal hunting grounds for promo men in search of hungry teenagers. Flyers, stickers, photographs, even free records, were distributed. By the time they'd finished, the hype alone was enough to guarantee pandemonium every time the Monkees' name was mentioned.

Last Train To Clarksville, the band's first single, was released three-and-a-half weeks before the TV show was premiered, and so masterfully had it all been planned that the Monkees came very close to topping both the Pop charts and the TV charts with their first shot at each. On September 9, 1966, the Monkees made their public debut, at New York's Broadway Theater. It was a curious performance; the band neither sang, played nor danced. They simply stood on the stage and introduced themselves. Three days later, NBC broadcast the first edition of the show.

The Monkees was unique in the annals of television, in that the plot was never anything more than an immediate by-product of the boys' own chemistry. Even the most asinine story lines never seemed premeditated; rather, watching The Monkees was like witnessing some absurd real life drama unfolding, and it didn't matter that you knew everything would turn out all right in the end, because the Monkees themselves were such happy-go-lucky sorts that it was surely only coincidence — or good fortune — that would see them win the day.

More importantly, the Monkees treated their audience as if they were equals. They had long hair, they wore the right clothes, they spoke the same language. They abused convention. They didn't go to school, they didn't work, their life was one long summer vacation. They just lived together and did what they liked together. They stood for rebellion. Not "Up against the wall" rebellion, but simple, adolescent rebellion.

They led a life no parent would have dreamed of mapping out for Junior. They dressed up and fell down, pulled faces, threw custard tarts, ran around and were as noisy as they liked. And there was never anybody to tell them not to ... nobody they listened to, at any rate.

As a formula, The Monkees could have run forever. In reruns, it probably will. The band itself, however, could not. The basic problem was that which Kasenatz-Katz were to circumnavigate by only using session men. Unfortunately, the very nature of The Monkees demanded they be visible, and it was not long before all four began hankering for a share of the limelight as performers in their own right, not as part of the phenomenon that was The Monkees.

Which is not to say that they wanted to break away from either the band or the show, not at first, anyway. But they did want more say in what went into the show, to project more of themselves and less of their mentors. Mike Nesmith's own artistic sensibilities had at least been acknowledged when Don Kirshner allowed him a couple of songs and a co-production credit on each of the band's first two albums. But the Monkees wanted more than that. They wanted to choose the songs they sang, to play on the songs they chose, options which had been closed to them from the moment Kirshner appeared on the set. Indeed, it was Kirshner who lay at the center of the dispute, and who was to remain there until, at the height of the argument, he released *A Little Bit Me, A Little Bit You* as a single, without consulting either the Monkees or Raybert.

He was ousted immediately, and while he later received what he described as the largest out of court settlement in the history of Columbia Pictures, the Monkees won something which, initially at least, was worth even more than money. They won their artistic freedom.

But well-meaning though Emil Viola and Lester Sill (the Monkees' new musical directors) were, even their acquiescence to the band's musical demands was not enough to give the Monkees the credibility they craved. Prior to Kirshner's departure, the band received considerable flak from within the industry when it was revealed that they didn't play on their own records. And while that was no big deal in itself, coupled with their other crimes — their manufactured origins, their callous manipulation of the marketplace, the fact that they hadn't paid their dues in the clubs and dives of America — it amounted to cardinal sin.

The publicity generated by Kirshner's departure eroded the Monkees' personal standing even more. Now they scarcely rated even as subordinates within the group and the show — everything was suddenly Don Kirshner. And while the credit he really deserves is, by itself, enormous, that which he then received surpassed everything.

The Monkees themselves belittled Kirshner's contributions, insisting that the power of their image was such that they would have succeeded whatever they did, and that the kids would be far better off with the music the Monkees themselves wanted to make. But there can be no doubt that, with Kirshner now out of the picture, the quality of band's musical output did begin to decline.

After two quite subliminal albums, THE MONKEES and MORE OF THE MONKEES, their third effort, HEADQUARTERS, was terribly patchy, a fate engendered largely by the inclusion of seven Monkee-made compositions. With the exceptions only of Nesmith's Beatles-ish *You Told Me* and Dolenz's *Randy Scouse Git* (a title the drummer picked up in England and, blissfully unaware of what it meant — Horny Jerk from Liverpool — selected for the band's next single), the band's own work for the most part was self-conscious and trite. *Band Six* was nothing more than a few seconds of frenzied neo-country music, *Zilch* a multi-layered Peter Piper tune over which each member recited a new line of gibberish before the whole thing degenerated into sinister, Zappa-esque whispers of "Zilch . . ."

Elsewhere, thankfully, sanity reigned on, with three Boyce / Hart compositions (most notably *Mr. Webster*), and Mann / Weill's gorgeous *Shades Of Gray*. But still, while the album effortlessly topped the chart in America, and reached number two in Britain, few people could honestly hold it up as a prime example of Monkee Business as it really should be sounding. PISCES, AQUARIUS, CAPRICORN AND JONES LTD., the fourth

Monkees' album, merely amplified these faults; HEAD, in November, 1968, screamed them out loud for the world to hear. The final flowering of the conceits which first raised their head on HEADQUARTERS, it was, quite simply, the Monkees' attempt to tell (and show; HEAD was also a movie) the world where they stood, politically, personally and publicly.

The movie opened to the sight of Mickey committing suicide while the soundtrack played Goffin / King's gorgeous *The Porpoise Song*, drifting from there into a series of only occasionally connected images whose main purpose was to parody the similarly sparse themes which ran through the television series. But the Monkees' audience didn't want parody, they wanted fun. HEAD gave them little of that, and with the TV series finally meeting its nemesis, the dog-days of the band, first as a Tork-less three piece, later as a simple Jones / Dolenz duo, could offer no solace to the generation who, having grown up in The Monkees' slipstream, now not only demanded, but expected, pop figureheads whom they could adore.

Because The Monkees went so far beyond the customary parameters of Rock and Roll idolatry, challenging even the Beatles' stranglehold, it mattered not that they appealed to what was primarily a pre-adolescent market. The devotion they received, and the money they earned, was no less real because of their audience's immaturity; indeed, the old adage of taking candy from a baby comes to mind ever more frequently, the more one considers The Monkees.

Exactly as had happened with the Beatles, Monkees' merchandising flooded the stores. But while the biggest thing Brian Epstein had ever marketed was a record store, The Monkees had the full promotional muscle of Columbia / Screen Gems behind them, and suddenly the stores were full of songbooks, games, toy guitars and drum kits, pins, pillow cases, posters, story books, tote bags, play-in-a-day guides (that one prompted a few ribald comments!), postcards, bubblegum . . . And they sold even faster than they could be manufactured (and still do, as a generation which grew up on The Monkees now recreates its childhood playpen through the auspices of internet auction houses, Rock and Roll memorabilia stores, garage sales, reissues and rehashes.)

It was another decade before such a full frontal assault was launched again, under the aegis of Kiss, whose painted ghastliness glared out from every surface it could be stuck to. But was the marketing machine idle in the mean time?

Does Tiffany still hang around shopping malls?

Discography:
Singles
- *Last Train To Clarksville / Take A Giant Step* (Colgems 1001, 1966)
- *I'm A Believer / Steppin' Stone* (Colgems 1002, 1966)
- *A Little Bit Me / She Hangs Out* (Colgems 1003, 1967)
- *A Little Bit Me / The Girl I Knew Somewhere* (Colgems 1004, 1967)
- *Pleasant Valley Sunday / Words* (Colgems 1007, 1967)
- *Daydream Believer / Goin' Down* (Colgems 1012, 1967)
- *Valleri / Tapioca Tundra* (Colgems 1019, 1968)
- *DW Washburn / It's Nice To Be With You* (Colgems 1023, 1968)
- *Porpoise Song / As We Go Along* (Colgems 1031, 1968)
- *Teardrop City / Man Without A Dream* (Colgems 5000, 1969)
- *Listen To The Band / Someday Man* (Colgems 5004, 1969)
- *Good Clean Fun / Mommy And Daddy* (Colgems 5005, 1969)
- *Oh My My / I Love You Better* (Colgems 5011, 1970)
- *Do It In The Name Of Love / Lady Jane* (Bell 986, 1971)

Albums
- THE MONKEES (Colgems 101, 1966)
- MORE OF THE MONKEES (Colgems 102, 1967)
- HEADQUARTERS (Colgems 103, 1967)
- PISCES, AQUARIUS, CAPRICORN & JONES LTD (Colgems 104, 1967)
- THE BIRDS, THE BEES & THE MONKEES (Colgems 109, 1968)
- HEAD (Colgems 5008, 1968)
- INSTANT REPLAY (Colgems 113, 1969)
- THE MONKEES' GREATEST HITS (Colgems 115, 1969)
- THE MONKEES PRESENT (Colgems 117, 1969)
- CHANGES (Colgems 119, 1970)

~ 7 ~
Dave Dee, Dozy, Beaky, Mick And Tich

1967: *Zabadak*

As Herman's Hermits' vaudevillian beat boom sensibilities were quick to prove, British bubblegum was always a far more eccentric beast than its American counterpart, if only because it was less tied down by its roots.

As in the US, the genre was spawned initially by so many novelty records, but while in America it was to exist almost as a twilight zone between lightweight humor and lowbrow pop, in Britain it would live happily alongside whatever else happened to be on display, and with few of the critical qualms which were to rock the boat Stateside.

Any number of reformed Beat Boom graduates — the Alan Price Set's *Simon Smith & His Amazing Dancing Bear*, the Tremoloes, even the Yardbirds, prowled the perimeter of the 'gum camp, but it was the ubiquitous Dave Dee, Dozy, Beaky, Mick & Tich who nailed precisely what bubblegum meant to the British, once visiting American GI's stopped giving it away to the girls — an impenetrable fog of such manic meaninglessness that, when the oddly named quintet came out with *Zabadak*, a British number 3 in November 1967, it was so damnably contagious, that it deserved a musical sub-heading all to itself. The title, incidentally, was rhymed with "Skag-a-lak," amongst other things.

The group formed in 1961, and though they turned professional quickly, Dave Dee and the Bostons were scarcely expecting to go top of the pops. Rather, their ambitions stretched little further than what Dee himself calls "the club and dance scene," and the beach front holiday camps where they spent their summers whipping holiday makers into a frenzy.

A gig in Swindon, opening for *Have I The Right* hit makers the Honeycombs, changed that, introducing the quintet to would-be managers Alan Blaikley and Ken Howard, and overwhelming them with the group's already dynamic statesmanship. And though few people believed that the band's name change to an eponymous mouthful could spell anything but disaster, things began moving quickly. In the four years between their first hit, *You Make It Move*, in November, 1965, and their last in 1969, Dave Dee, Dozy, Beaky, Mick and Tich spent 141 weeks on the British chart. During that same period, the Beatles managed just 139.

Created under the almost maniacal vision of producer Steve Rowlands, the majority of the band's music was recorded in an almost frighteningly slapdash fashion. *Bend It*, which began as a gentle waltz and ended as a Cossack barn dance, was simply the band putting to good use a bugbear which afflicts many groups — the problem of staying in tempo for a whole three minutes.

The Legend Of Xanadu was cut in just half an hour with an untried engineer, and boasted realistic whip sounds created by dragging a beer bottle down a fret board, then smacking two bits of wood together. The band may have been subject to perpetual abuse from the serious rock establishment, especially once their experiments began moving in the direction of the burgeoning psychedelic movement, but in terms of musical inventiveness, Dave Dee, Dozy, Beaky, Mick, Tich and producer Steve Rowlands were closer to the edge than any of their more eclectic peers.

Visually, too, the band were streets ahead of the rest of the pack, promoting full-blown costume spectaculars which weren't to be fully equaled until the advent of Adam & The Ants in 1980. History's refusal to acknowledge the band as anything more than a tacky pop extravaganza, whose greatest claim to fame was their use of earthy language on stage, was an injustice which Adam, alone, was to rectify. But what was good for the goose was not necessarily good for the gander, and behind the scenes, Rowlands, Howard and Blaikley were adamant that they would not be tarred with the same brush for long.

Discography:
Singles
  ○ *You Make It Move / No Time* (Fontana 1537, 1966)
  ○ *Hold Tight / You Know What I Want* (Fontana 1545, 1966)
  ○ *Hideaway / Here's A Heart* (Fontana 1553, 1966)

- ° *Bend It / She's So Good* (Fontana 1559, 1966)
- ° *Save Me / Shame* (Fontana 1569, 1967)
- ° *Okay / Master Llewellyn* (Fontana 1591, 1967)
- ° *Zabadak / The Sun Goes Down* (Imperial 66270, 1967)
- ° *Legend Of Xanadu / Please* (Imperial 66287, 1968)

Albums
- ° GREATEST HITS (Fontana 67567, 1967)

~ 8 ~
The Herd

1967: *From The Underworld*

Though Peter Frampton's fame and name rest today upon the multi-million selling double album FRAMPTON COMES ALIVE, released in 1975 and still one of the biggest selling LP's of all time, his success was by no means overnight, nor even particularly unexpected. Eight years earlier, after all, Frampton had been riding a wave of similarly seismic proportions, charting high across Europe with some of the most remarkable pop hits of the late 1960's, and celebrating with a personal title which still echoes with all the exuberance and naivety of those innocent days. He was, Britain's pop papers insisted, "the Face Of '68," and gazing back upon the boyish features, the choirboy smile, the dashing good looks which were Frampers' in abundance . . . you can see why.

Born in Beckenham, England, and schooled alongside the young David Bowie, Frampton was the leader of the Herd, whose 1967-68 hits *From The Underworld, Paradise Lost* and *I Don't Want Our Loving To Die* remain among the most insistently individual hits of the age, darkly atmospheric, emotionally evocative, and absolutely heartbreaking. The fact that Frampton himself didn't even expect to be a singer, let alone a teen pop idol, only adds a charming piquancy to the whole affair.

Already a guitarist of some local, south-east London, renown, Frampton was still in his early teens when he first encountered the Herd, a neighborhood R&B band formed by Tony Chapman, best remembered then as the original drummer with the Rolling Stones. Andy Bown (keyboards), Gary Taylor (guitar), bassist Louie (later of Renaissance), and a singer whom Frampton recalls only as "Terry someone" completed the line-up, "and I used to go see them all the time." He struck up a friendship, and when Chapman quit to form a new band, the Preachers, Frampton was asked to join.

Throughout all this, Chapman's mentor was the Stones' Bill Wyman. Having already encouraged the Herd to record Jagger & Richards' *So Much In Love* as a single, Wyman then took the Preachers under his wing, both as manager and co-producer. But a single, *Hole In My Soul*, and a spot on TV's READY STEADY GO the night the Stones took over hosting the show, did nothing to raise the band's profile, and by late 1965, the Preachers had metamorphosed into Moon's Train, a blues / soul revue modeled on the more successful Steampacket. But that, too, fizzled out after a few high hopes, and when Frampton next surfaced, he was a member of the Herd.

"When they we got rid of Terry, the singer guy, everybody switched around. Louis was in the band a little longer, then Gary switched to bass, and I became guitarist. I joined as rhythm guitarist, ended up as lead guitarist within a very short space of time, and all of a sudden everything started happening."

A summer 1966 residency at London's famed Marquee Club saw the Herd's psychedelic blues winning them any number of rave plaudits, and a new manager, Steve Rowlands. He took the Herd to the Ken Howard / Alan Blaikley song writing team with whom he had long been working and said "you'll do some demos for us, which we did. Then they looked down the line, came to me and said 'you'll sing'."

Up to this point, Andy Bown had handled all the band's vocals, but his position behind the organ was hardly the strongest visual presence a group could have. The Herd knew this, but still, Frampton demurred. "I said 'no no no, you don't understand, I'm the new guy, I do what they tell me, I just play guitar and do oohs and aahs.' But they said, 'no no no, YOU don't understand. If you want a hit, you'll be the singer, and the others went 'b-b-b-but . . . oh all right then.' And that was it."

Thanks to Dave Dee, Dozy, Beaky, Mick & Tich; Ken Howard, Alan Blaikley and Steve Rowlands were the hot team of the day, hampered only the critics' total disdain for every last inch of their art. The Herd, then, was to be the answer to their ambitious dreams, a point which was proved when the group's debut single under the new team's aegis, the effects drenched *I Can Fly*, earned a batch of good reviews, then flopped with disarming ease.

Knowing, however, that they were onto a good thing, and that promotion alone stood in the band's way, Howard / Blaikley completely realigned the Herd's image around Frampton's youthful good looks. According to legend, it was during the last few vital moments before the Herd went on television that Frampton's transformation from blues guitarist to teenybop idol was accomplished. The singer was wandering around the studio in jeans and sweater, and Howard was horrified. He raided the studio wardrobe department, but there was nothing to be found. Still there was no way Frampton could go on TV looking like he'd been dressed by his mother.

Finally, Howard found inspiration. Grabbing a pair of scissors, he physically attacked Frampton's sweater, cutting squares out of the torso and then completing the look by removing one shoulder. Fifteen years before FLASHDANCE, it was, Howard later swore, "a mini-sensation. Everybody talked about it. We got letters. Kids were seen shortly afterwards wearing similar garments. Talk about image!"

The Herd's next single was *From The Underworld*, an adaptation of the Greek legend of Orpheus which not only proved one of the most memorable singles of the year, it was also one of the weirdest. Opening with a tolling bell and a mournful piano, an explosive guitar ushers in the monkish chanting over which Frampton, sounding considerably more desolate than any 17 year old has a right to, mourns his fate. Add a brass section, an orchestra, and more crashing guitar, and you have a performance even Meatloaf, at his BAT OUT OF HELL-shaped overkill best, could not have surpassed (although it would be great to hear him try.)

copyright 1987 Phil Anderson / KAOS2000 Magazine

A later era Peter Frampton playing guitar for David Bowie on the 1987 Tour

Fontana, the band's label, was mortified. "They didn't think it was commercial," Howard later said. "But Alan and I really believed in that song, mainly because we'd been to the same school and had done Virgil's *Orpheus In The Underworld* as a set text in Latin. We'd gone to some trouble to transform it into a pop song, keeping many of the original allusions. It was totally lost on the record buying public, but we liked it."

With pirate radio DJ Alan Freeman throwing all his (not inconsiderable) influence behind the song, *From The Underworld* soared to No. 6 that summer of 1967, with the similarly themed, swing inflected *Paradise Lost* (John Milton was the classical inspiration this time) following. An even more extravagant sonic excursion, it faltered at No. 15, however, an unexpectedly lowly fate which also greeted the Herd's first album.

The Herd bounced back in the spring of 1968, with their fourth single, and their biggest hit ever. The distinctly Dave Dee-esque *I Don't Want Our Loving To Die* reached No. 5 and was directly responsible for the British teen press leaping aboard the Frampton bandwagon. RAVE magazine proclaimed him "The Face of '68," the teen dream sensation of the year; the 18 year old's face stared out from a million bedroom wall pin ups. In a year when pop stars were growing ever more hirsute and hippy, Frampton was a breath of clean shaven freshness. And he hated it.

"We realized he had a fantastic face for photographs," Howard recalled. "He was a very good looking kid. As soon as he assumed the lead, we started selling records. [But] he got this great fan following which was terrifying for him. He used to weep and sob. I felt terribly sorry for him; he wasn't ready for it, didn't want it, couldn't cope."

The Herd's relationship with both Howard / Blaikley and Steve Rowlands, too, was cracking, and as 1968 continued, former Stones manager Andrew Oldham and partner Tony Calder took over the group's management. Their first move was to remove the Herd from all accusations of being another Howard / Blaikley puppet, by allowing Frampton and Andy Bown to write the band's next A-side, *Sunshine Cottage*. Unfortunately, attempts to ride Frampton's acclaim up the charts failed abysmally. A duet between Frampton's pure pop voice and Bown's more sonorous tones, *Sunshine Cottage* simply dropped out of sight the moment it hit the streets.

The Herd followed. When Oldham / Calder failed to work out, the group transferred to Mindbenders manager Harvey Lisburg, only for him to drop them after just three months. Frampton was already talking with Steve Marriott about forming a new band, Humble Pie; Bown was looking towards a solo career . . . by late 1968, the Herd had sundered, and the Face of 68 never looked back.

Discography:
Singles
- *I Can Fly* / *Understand Me* (Fontana 1588, 1967)
- *From The Underworld* / *Sweet William* (Fontana 1602, 1967)
- *Paradise Lost* / *Come On, Believe Me* (Fontana 1610, 1967)
- *I Don't Want Our Loving To Die* / *Our Fairy Tale* (Fontana 1618, 1968)
- *The Game* / *Beauty Queen* (Fontana 1646, 1968)
Albums
- LOOKIN' THRU YOU (Fontana 67579, 1968)

~ 9 ~
The Bee Gees

1967: *Massachussetts*

While America was getting ever higher on Bubblegum, and the UK was chewing the cud of its own peculiar variations, Australia, too, was embracing the delights of lustrous, livid pop music, courtesy of three teenaged immigrants named the Bee Gees.

Going on to become one of the longest-surviving groups in pop history, the Bee Gees can also claim a place among the most eclectic. Through the 1960's, they were widely regarded as the heirs to the Beatles' throne of lushly produced and extraordinarily literate pop. Into the 1970's, and they became prime purveyors of the disco boom; through the 1980's they experimented with sensitive AOR; and in the 1990's, they balanced their logical standing as a nostalgia machine with a continuing (if slower) stream of classy recordings and triumphant live performances. In fact, the only things which didn't change were the magnificent melodies, and close, high harmonies which had been the Bee Gees' trademark since the beginning.

The Bee Gees' name, of course, was an abbreviation of the Brothers Gibb — vocalist / guitarist Barry Gibb, and the younger twins Robin and Maurice. All three were born in England, Barry in Manchester, the twins on the Isle Of Man, and in 1955 the trio made their performing debut as the Blue Cats, opening for their band leader father at a Manchester club with a short set of skiffle numbers.

The family moved to Brisbane, Australia, in 1958, and — as the Brothers Gibb — the boys immediately graduated to the local talent contest circuit. By the following year, disc jockey Bill Gates had discovered them, and was regularly airing their demos on his radio show, exposure which led, in turn, to an 18 month residency at the Beachcomber Nightclub in Surfers Paradise.

In 1962, the Brothers Gibb signed to Festival Records, landed their own television series, and embarked upon a string of classic Australian hits, beginning with *The Battle Of The Blue And Grey*, in March, 1963. Heavily influenced by the Merseybeat sounds creeping over from the UK, of course, the now abbreviated Bee Gees were nevertheless carving out a sound that was uniquely their

The Bee Gees

own, and by 1964, both their ambition and their abilities were on display for all to see: *Claustrophobia, Theme From The Travels Of Jamie McPheeters* and *The House Without Windows* each rate alongside any Cavern Clubber's contemporary output, and by the time of their debut album, BARRY GIBB AND THE BEE GEES SING AND PLAY 14 BARRY GIBB SONGS, the group was already looking towards returning to England, to try their luck there.

The Bee Gees' Australian adventures culminated in September, 1966 with *Spicks And Specks*, an Australian chart topper and the title track of their second album. By early 1967, the three brothers plus bassist Vince Melouney and drummer Colin Peterson were in London, under the managerial aegis of the legendary Robert Stigwood. A deal with Polydor followed, and in April, the doom-laden *New York Mining Disaster 1941* (since covered by anarchist hitmakers Chumbawamba) gave the Bee Gees a Top 20 hit in both Britain and the US.

To Love Somebody, a song later covered by everyone from Janis Joplin to John Otway, followed, together with a deceptively titled third album, BEE GEES FIRST. But it was with their next hit, the gorgeous *Massachusetts*, that the Bee Gees truly hit their commercial stride. Their first British chart topper, it opened the floodgates for a wealth of exquisite melodies — *World, Words, I've Got To Get A Message To You* (another No. 1), *I Started A Joke* and *First Of May* (theme to the smash movie "S.W.A.L.K."), a sublime streak which not only established the Bee Gees among the most justly respected performers of the era, but also confirmed their ascendancy up the teenybop stakes. The toothsome trio may not have been classically handsome, but to a teenaged following still reeling from Peter Frampton's decision to go "heavy" with Humble Pie, the Bee Gees were primal pin-up material. When Maurice married singer Lulu in 1969, the scene was swamped by sobbing teenyboppers.

The trio's singles unashamedly catered to this audience. Their albums, on the other hand, evinced a maturity and seriousness which surely baffled the little girls. Both IDEA and the sprawling double ODESSA bathed their feet in the then prevalent pools of psychedelia — and more than their feet as well. In mid-1969, with the band riven by drug and alcohol problems, Robin quit for a solo career and immediately scored a hit with *Saved By The Bell*.

A messy lawsuit involving drummer Peterson added to Barry and Maurice's woes, while a new album, the soundtrack to the movie CUCUMBER CASTLE, saw their British

The Bee Gees

commercial stock plummet as well. The Bee Gees didn't score a single top 10 hit in Britain between *Don't Forget To Remember*, in August, 1969, and *Run To Me*, in July, 1972. In America, however, their ever maturing country rock ballad sound found them a whole new audience, and with the errant Robin now back in the fold, the brothers scored two of their biggest hits yet: *Lonely Days* (a No. 3 in November, 1970) and 1971's chart-topping *How Can You Mend A Broken Heart.*

But the albums TRAFALGAR, TO WHOM IT MAY CONCERN and LIFE IN A TIN CAN faltered badly, and with successive singles likewise going down the dumper, by 1973 the Bee Gees were reduced to the American club circuit, and were all but utterly meaningless in the UK. Manager Stigwood, however, was not sitting idly by while his charges' career stumbled to a halt. Aware that many of the Bee Gees' problems stemmed from the simple fact that they were no longer considered hip, Stigwood decided to return to a promotional ploy that he had first employed seven years earlier for *New York Mining Disaster, 1941*, mailing out copies of their next single to radio stations in plain sleeves, with a plain white label. An accompanying note asked only that the record be played and judged by its contents. If you played it and liked it, you'd be told who it was. If you didn't, then it didn't matter, did it? By the time the artist's identity became common knowledge, *Jive Talking* was already on its way to No. 1.

Jive Talking, and the album from which it was taken, the Arif Marden produced MAIN COURSE, showcased a whole new direction for the group, abandoning the harmonic pop of the past for an earthy, dance-inflected sound which even Rolling Stone described as "approach[ing] disco without straying too far from established pop conventions." By July, 1976, the Bee Gees had returned to the Top 10 album charts, and were celebrating a new No. 1, *You Should Be Dancing.*

The Bee Gees were in France, recording at the Chateau d'Heureville, when Stigwood approached them about the SATURDAY NIGHT FEVER soundtrack. According to Barry Gibb, his message was vague at best. "We want four songs for this film." They asked him what it was about. "A bunch of guys that live in New York," he replied. Later, of course, he expanded on that, even mentioned that it was a disco-based movie. But the band never did see a script.

The first songs to be completed were *If I Can't Have You*, and an older number called *Saturday Night, Saturday Night*, which eventually metamorphosed into *Staying Alive.* "There are so many bloody records out called *Saturday Night*, Maurice apologized when Stigwood complained that the original name was better. "It's corny, it's a terrible title." And if the impresario didn't like the change, Maurice added, the band would keep the song for themselves. Stigwood liked the change.

What happened next was extraordinary. The gentle *How Deep Is Your Love* was the first hit from the soundtrack, and still romping towards the top of the charts in September, 1977, when its follow-up, *Staying Alive*, was unleashed. It, too, went to No. 1, while the movie soundtrack would top the charts for 24 weeks. In January, 1978, *Night Fever* made it three chart-toppers on the trot, granting the Bee Gees a supremacy which was only emphasized when it became obvious that the only records that could knock them off the top were others with which they were indelibly associated: Yvonne Elliman's version of *If*

I Can't Have You, which they wrote; Player's *Baby Come Back*, which shared both their label and their sound; and younger brother Andy's *(Love Is) Thicker Than Water*.

Indeed, Andy, too, chalked up consecutive number ones with three successive singles. Even more incredibly, the Bee Gees' own next three singles were also chart-toppers, adding up to a dominance which made even the Beatles' achievements pale in comparison. Sales of SATURDAY NIGHT FEVER itself, meantime, would not be bettered until Michael Jackson's genre-busting THRILLER finally overhauled it in 1984. Still, it sold over 25 million copies, establishing it as the best-selling soundtrack album of all time, with sales of 1996's remastered CD edition improving on that figure all the time.

ENTIRE 2-RECORD SET   8T-2-4200

In 1978, the Bee Gees starred (alongside Peter Frampton) in Stigwood's film musical version of the Beatles' SGT. PEPPER'S LONELY HEARTS CLUB BAND, a comparative failure, but still a reasonable musical triumph. 1979's SPIRITS HAVING FLOWN returned them to the top of the charts, both in its own right and via three successive singles, *Tragedy, Too Much Heaven* and *Love You Inside Out.* The disco bubble which the Bee Gees epitomized, however, was bursting, and after 1981's LIVING EYES became an utterly unexpected flop, the Bee Gees effectively ceased recording, moving behind the scenes to write and produce hits for brother Andy, Barbra Streisand, Diana Ross, Dionne Warwick and so on.

They returned in 1987 with ESP, a musical rebirth and yet another commercial renaissance. America wasn't buying, but elsewhere around the world, both the album and the *You Win Again* 45 were chart-toppers, an achievement which 1989's ONE duplicated. 1991's HIGH CIVILIZATION, 1993's SIZE ISN'T EVERYTHING and 1997's STILL WATERS, all evidencing the team's continued grasp of great adult pop, followed, and in 1997, the Bee Gees were inducted into the Rock and Roll Hall of Fame. But their admission to its (as yet unfounded) Pop cousin, needless to say, was achieved long before.

Discography:
Singles
- *New York Mining Disaster 1941 / Can't see Nobody* (Atco 6487, 1967)
- *To Love Somebody / Close Another Door* (Atco 6503, 1967)
- *Holiday / Every Christian Lion Hearted Man* (Atco 6521, 1967)
- *Massachusetts / Sir Geoffrey Saved The World* (Atco 6532, 1967)

- *Words / Sinking Ships* (Atco 6548, 1968)
- *Jumbo / The Singer Sang His Song* (Atco 6570, 1968)
- *Gotta Get A Message To You / Kitty Can* (Atco 6603, 1968)
- *I Started A Joke / Kilburn Towers* (Atco 6639, 1969)
- *First Of May / Lamplight* (Atco 6657, 1969)
- *Tomorrow Tomorrow / Sun In My Morning* (Atco 6682, 1969)
- *Don't Forget To Remember / Lay Down And Die* (Atco 6702, 1969)
- *If Only I Had My Mind On Something Else / Sweetheart* (Atco 6741, 1970)
- *IOIO / Then You Left Me* (Atco 6752, 1970)
- *Lonely Days / Man For All Seasons* (Atco 6795, 1971)
- *How Can you Mend A Broken Heart / Country Woman* (Atco 6824, 1971)
- *Don't Wanna Live Inside Myself / Walking Back* (Atco 6847, 1971)
- *My World / On Time* (Atco 6871, 1972)
- *Run To Me / Road To Alaska* (Atco 6896, 1972)
- *Alive / Paper Mache Cabbages And Kings* (Atco 6909, 1972)
- *Saw A New Morning / My Life Has Been A Song* (RSO 401, 1973)
- *Wouldn't It Be Someone / Elisa* (RSO 404, 1973)
- *Mr Natural / It Doesn't Matter Much Anymore* (RSO 408, 1974)
- *Throw A Penny / I Can't Let Go* (RSO 410, 1974)
- *Charade / Heavy Breathing* (RSO 501, 1974)
- *Jive Talkin' / Wind Of Change* (RSO 510, 1975)
- *Nights On Broadway / Edge Of The Universe* (RSO 515, 1975)
- *Fanny / Country Lanes* (RSO 519, 1975)
- *You Should Be Dancing / Subway* (RSO 853, 1976)
- *Love So Right / You Stepped Into My Life* (RSO 859, 1976)
- *Boogie Child / Lovers* (RSO 867, 1976)
- *Edge Of The Universe / Words* (RSO 880, 1977)
- *How Deep Is Your Love / Can't Keep A Good Man Down* (RSO 882, 1977)
- *Stayin' Alive / If I Can't Have You* (RSO 885, 1977)
- *Night Fever / Down The Road* (RSO 889, 1978)
- *She's Leaving Home / Oh Darling* (RSO 907, 1978)
- *Too Much Heaven / Rest Your Love On Me* (RSO 913, 1978)
- *Tragedy / Until* (RSO 918, 1979)
- *Love You Inside Out / I'm Satisfied* (RSO 925, 1979)
- *He's A Liar / (instrumental)* (RSO 1066, 1981)
- *Living Eyes / I Still Love You* (RSO 1067, 1981)
- *The Woman In You / Stayin' Alive* (RSO 813-373, 1983)
- *Someone Belonging To Someone / I Love You Too Much* (Warner Bros 815-235, 1983)
- *ESP / Overnight* (Warner Bros 28139, 1987)
- *You Win Again / Backtafunk* (Warner Bros 28351, 1987)
- *You Win Again / Will You Ever Let Me* (Warner Bros 22733, 1989)
- *One / Wing And A Prayer* (Warner Bros 22889, 1989)
- *Paying The Price Of Love / (remixes)* (Polydor 859164, 1993)
- *Alone / How Deep Is Your Love* (Polydor 1006, 1997)

Albums
- ° BEE GEES FIRST (Atco 223, 1967)
- ° HORIZONTAL (Atco 233, 1968)
- ° IDEA (Atco 253, 1968)
- ° RARE PRECIOUS AND BEAUTIFUL (Atco 264, 1968)
- ° BEST OF (Atco 292, 1969)
- ° ODESSA (Atco 702, 1969)
- ° RARE PRECIOUS AND BEAUTIFUL VOLUME TWO (Atco 321, 1970)
- ° CUCUMBER CASTLE (Atco 327, 1970)
- ° TWO YEARS ON (Atco 353, 1971)
- ° TRAFALGAR (Atco 7003, 1971)
- ° TO WHOM IT MAY CONCERN (Atco 7012, 1972)
- ° LIFE IN A TIN CAN (RSO 870, 1973)
- ° BEST OF VOLUME TWO (RSO 875, 1973)
- ° MR. NATURAL (RSO 4800, 1974)
- ° CHILDREN OF THE WORLD (RSO 3003, 1976)
- ° MAIN COURSE (RSO 3024, 1977)
- ° HERE AT LAST ... LIVE (RSO 3901, 1977)
- ° SPIRITS HAVING FLOWN (RSO 3041, 1979)
- ° GREATEST (RSO 4200, 1979)
- ° LIVING EYES (RSO 3098, 1981)
- ° STAYING ALIVE (RSO 813269, 1983)
- ° ESP (Warner Bros. 25541, 1987)
- ° ONE (Warner Bros. 25887, 1989)
- ° SIZE ISN'T EVERYTHING (Polydor 521055, 1993)
- ° STILL WATERS (Polydor 537302, 1997)
- ° ONE NIGHT ONLY (Polydor 559220, 1998)

~ 10 ~
The Cowsills

1967: *The Rain, The Park And Other Things*

The Cowsills emerged in mid-1967 as the first, and in many ways the prototypical, family of pop. The Bee Gees, after all, were brothers alone. The Cowsills spanned two generations, the wife (Barbara), daughter (Susan), and four sons (Bill, Bob, Paul, Barry and John) of an ex-Navy officer from Rhode Island, and from the start, their wholesome appeal was inescapable.

The Rain, The Park And Other Things, their first hit single that fall, encapsulated everything there was to know about the Cowsills, an inoffensive Boy Meets Girl (In The Park, In The Rain) ditty which tore up the Top 40, and almost unwittingly served up a role model for every pop family of the next five years. Television's Partridge Family was based unapologetically upon their story, while both the Osmonds and the Jackson Five borrowed heavily from the Cowsills' own marketing approach — including the drive to ensure that the youngest of the family was constantly being propelled into the spotlight, while its elders maintained a studied distance, the whole bunch coming together chiefly to propound the joys of family life.

In many ways they put one in mind of Pat Boone, or any of those other grisly whiter than white, cuter than cute manifestations of 50's Americana. Certainly, they were the perfect antidote to the Youth Rebellion of the late 1960's; clean living kids who loved their mom so much they would even get up on stage with her. Imagine the Jefferson Airplane doing that.

Yet it was their very wholesomeness which was to destroy the Cowsills. They broadcast the delights of a chemical-free diet several years before their audience was ready for it, and having made it as Official Spokes-singers for the milk marketing industry, when their appeal began to fade they sacrificed every last iota of integrity by recording the version of *Hair* which gave them their fourth, and final, Top 40 hit in March 1969.

The Cowsills struggled on for a little longer, broke up and then reformed (following mother Barbara's death) in the early 1990's. But the true measure of their import was drawn two decades earlier, first with the all-America explosion of bubbly bubblegum pop, and then with the worldwide fireball of families which followed. And though it might be a little over-zealous to describe the Cowsills as being ahead of their time . . . what other explanation is there for all of that?

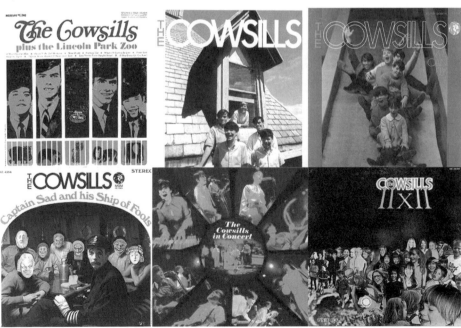

Discography:
Singles
- *All I Really Want / And The Next Day, Too* (Joda 103, 1965)
- *Most Of All / Siamese Cat* (Philips 40382, 1966)
- *Party Girl / What's It Gonna Be Like?* (Philips 40406, 1966)
- *A Most Peculiar Man / Could It Be?* (Philips 40437, 1967)
- *Rain, The Park & Other Things / River Blue* (MGM 13810, 1967)
- *We Can Fly / Time For Remembrance* (MGM 13886, 1967)
- *In Need Of A Friend / Mr. Flynn* (MGM 13909, 1968)
- *Indian Lake / Newspaper Blanket* (MGM 13944, 1968)
- *Poor Baby / Meet Me At The Wishing Well* (MGM 13981, 1968)
- *Captain Sad & His Ship Of Fools / Path Of Love* (MGM 14003, 1968)
- *The Candy Kid / Impossible Years* (MGM 14011, 1969)
- *Hair / What Is Happy?* (MGM 14026, 1969)
- *Prophecy Of Daniel & John The Divine / Gotta Get Away* (MGM 14063, 1969)
- *Love, American Style / Silver Threads & Golden Needles* (MGM 14084, 1969)
- *11 x 11 / Start To Love* (MGM 14106, 1970)
- *On My Side / There Is A Child* (London 149, 1971)
- *You /* (London 153, 1971)
- *Covered Wagon / Blue Road* (London 170, 1971)

Albums
- PLUS THE LINCOLN PARK ZOO (Wing 16354, 1967)
- COWSILLS (MGM 4498, 1967)
- WE CAN FLY (MGM 4534, 1967)
- CAPTAIN SAD & HIS SHIP OF FOOLS (MGM 4554, 1968)
- THE BEST OF THE COWSILLS (MGM 4597, 1969)
- IN CONCERT (MGM 4619, 1968)
- 11 x 11 (MGM 4639, 1970)
- ALL TIME HITS (MGM 103, 1971)
- ON MY SIDE (London 587, 1970)

~ 11 ~
The Music Explosion

1967: *Little Bit O'Soul*

Neil Bogart's chief claim to fame had been a smattering of long-forgotten mid-west pop stardom in the guise of Neil Scott, Teen Idol. It didn't last, but Bogart never really intended it too. Rather, he saw his future on the other side of the entrepreneurial desk, as Mark Stein — later a member of mogadon pomp quartet Vanilla Fudge — discovered a little later. "When I was 11 ... my dad got me into a Rock and Roll show, emceed by Neil, who had a song (*Bobby*) in the charts. He became my manager. I was 11 and Neil was 16."

Since then, Bogart had moved up to become Vice President of Cameo Records, one half of Cameo Parkway, but for many years, the poorer half. While Parkway launched Chubby Checker and the Twist, Cameo struggled on with a sporadic series of turntable hits and the odd regional breaker, and when Bogart picked up on another local hit, *96 Tears* by the mysterious ? And The Mysterions, few folks expected his luck to change.

Instead the song gave Cameo their first ever No. 1, and while neither Cameo, Bogart nor the Mysterions were ever to repeat that one great success, Bogart was suddenly established as a man with a finger on the pulse. And during the summer of 1967, he proved it with the recruitment of two studio whiz kids, Jerry Kasenatz and Jeff Katz, to Cameo. What happened next, as they say, would become history.

Natives of Long Island, the pair had been working together for a little under eighteen months, primarily with low-key proto-punk outfits whose efforts were for the most part not even to leave the studio. When they did, they sank. Rare Breed, who debuted the duo's production talents in the marketplace, chalked up two resounding zeros in a row, first with *Beg, Borrow And Steal*, a frantic adaptation of the basic *Louie Louie* riff, spiced up with a few nice hooklines, then with *Come On Down To My Boat (Baby)*.

Shortly after that, the Music Explosion's *Little Black Egg* failed to hatch, but within a year, Kasenatz-Katz were riding high in the chart, both in their own right (The Music Explosion's *Little Bit O'Soul*) and by proxy, when Every Mother's Son took their own version of *Come On Down To My Boat* into the Top Ten.

Little Bit O'Soul was the crystallization, in embryonic form at least, of everything Kasenatz-Katz had been working towards in the garages and back rooms of their east coast stomping ground. Their earlier efforts, after all, revolved primarily around the dexterous reproduction of innumerable proto-punk archetypes, crammed together in an uneasy alliance of sloppiness and pomp. This time, however, the duo loosened up a little, allowing vocalist Jimmy Lyons more room in which to maneuver, and providing the rhythm section — Butch Stahl and Bob Avery — with a beat even Moulty, The Barbarians' hook-handed drummer, could have tapped out in his sleep.

The Music Explosion

Although Kasenatz-Katz's career was still very much in its infancy, Neil Bogart was swift to win an introduction to them. He sensed an immediate chemistry. When Kasenatz-Katz spoke of their ambitions, he saw his own being spelt out before him. They wanted to create a sound as individual as Phil Spector's, as dynamic as Andrew Oldham's, as instantly recognizable as Lieber-Stoller's, and somehow Bogart knew that if anybody was entitled to such lofty aims, it was these earnest, likable young New Yorkers.

For Kasenatz-Katz, Bogart was the only man they'd met who offered them exactly the terms they wanted — the promise of being able to work in any way they wished, with the minimum of bureaucratic interference. They had a dream, but it was an exclusive one. They wanted to build an empire in which the sound, the groups, the music and the marketing were as one. All they needed was the money to pay for it, and a backer with the belief to stand by them even if success was not immediately apparent.

In any event, their first effort for Cameo was a hit. Confident that the failure of *Beg, Borrow And Steal* had been due almost entirely to their having tried introducing their techniques to the marketplace a little at a time, rather than in one all-embracing, devastating single blow, they virtually rebuilt *Little Bit O'Soul* around the Ohio Express' interpretation of *Beg, Borrow And Steal*. And by the end of November, they had another hit on their hands.

Discography:
Singles
- *Little Black Egg* / *Stay By My Side* (Attack 1404, 1966)
- *Little Bit O'Soul* / *I See The Light* (Laurie 3380, 1966)
- *Sunshine Games* / *Can't Stop Now* (Laurie 3400, 1967)
- *We Gotta Go Home* / *Hearts & Flowers* (Laurie 3414, 1967)
- *What You Want* / *Roadrunner* (Laurie 3429, 1967)
- *Where Are We Going?* / *Flash* (Laurie 3440, 1968)
- *Yes Sir* / *Dazzling* (Laurie 3454, 1968)
- *Jack In The Box* / *Rewind* (Laurie 3466, 1969)
- *What's Your Name?* / *Calling Me Anything* (Laurie 3479, 1969)
- *Little Black Egg* / *Stay By My Side* (Laurie 3500, 1969)

Albums
- LITTLE BIT O'SOUL (Laurie 2040, 1967)

~ 12 ~
The Ohio Express

1968: *Yummy Yummy Yummy*

The Ohio Express, like the Music Explosion, were primarily a studio-based outfit, comprising Dale Powers (vocals), Doug Grassel (guitar), Dean Kastran (bass), Jim Pfayler (keyboards) and Tim Corwin (drums.) They operated out of Mansfield, Ohio, and legend had it that they rehearsed in a deserted railroad station. One night a huge crowd gathered around them, but not — as the band thought — to listen to them. Rather, the Ohio Express, a super-fast freight train, was due through, and everybody wanted to get a look at it. The band immediately renamed themselves after the train in the hope that people would find them as exciting as the puff puff evidently was.

In truth, the name — like the band itself — was simply another of Kasenatz-Katz's inventions. A ready-made band would have been of little use to them, they required intransigence, the knowledge that anybody they chose could play for the Express. They chose Rare Breed. Their vision of artistic control simply could not be fulfilled if they had to deal with regular musicians, with all the ego trips and demands that that would involve. Session men, on the other hand, might not enjoy playing what they were given, but at least they would play it, and play it well.

The success of *Beg, Borrow And Steal* was followed by a surprising flop, *Try It*, but label head Neil Bogart remained unperturbed, and when he left Cameo for his own Buddah label, he was not slow to offer Kasenatz-Katz similar freedoms within the new company to those they had enjoyed at the old — something Cameo's next president, Allen Klein, was unlikely to have agreed to.

Buddah was established primarily as a Light (as opposed to Easy) Listening label, a principle borne out by the company's first chart success, the Lemon Piper's *Green Tambourine*. Of course Bogart could not expect to have the entire market to himself. What was to set Buddah apart was the guile with which that market would be courted. With the exception only of a handful of licensed British acts (Buddah later acquired distribution rights to the British Progressive Rock independent, Charisma), nothing even remotely threatening was to sully Buddah's name. Even Crazy Elephant, Kasenatz-Katz's brilliant concession to the growing "Heavy" market, were farmed out to the Bell label. Faced with so many possibilities, so much potential, Bogart simply knew that the aims with which he founded Buddah would be successful.

Although the summer of '67 has gone down in the annals of history as that of Psychedelia, it's only in retrospect that the splintered scenes which existed in London and 'Frisco can be seen as two divergent streams. American pop was still struggling to reestablish itself after the British Invasion, and with Herman's Hermits' peculiar hybrid of English music hall standards and equally innocent sub-beat boppers still holding the pre-teens in their sweatless grasp, American business was still more concerned with manufacturing a homegrown response to the likes of them, than attempting to stem, or cash in on, the activities of a handful of hippies on the streets of San Francisco. That would come later, because really, what was the more important record: Jefferson Airplane's *White Rabbit*? Or the Ohio Express' second smash hit *Yummy Yummy Yummy*.

Alongside Herman's *Sunshine Girl*, a simultaneous hit in Britain even if America was to all but ignore it (it made No. 101, the band's worst showing yet), *Yummy* was to launch the western world into a summer of Bubblegum. Yet it's a season which seems to have passed most rock historians by. Serious rock fans lifted their musical preferences from the pages of the serious rock press, the serious rock press thus lifts its memories from the recollections of the serious rock fans.

The Jefferson Airplane, the Grateful Dead, the Doors and Big Brother were the conscience of the age; everything else was inconsequential pap, marketed and manufactured for an audience whose collective IQ barely reached room temperature. But really, who was kidding who?

The key to any such argument along these lines lies in the definition of the term Pop Music. The division between Pop and Rock, between what was "acceptable" and what was not, had grown immense over the last couple of years. According to the growing wave of "serious" music critics which had emerged to keep the musicians company, pop was no longer an abbreviation of "Popular"; now it suggested something so wholesome it was unwholesome, something which crept into your house while you slept, cleansed your spirit, corrupted your sister and left a sticky trail of slime everywhere it went. It appealed to the idiot masses and led them, sheep-like, into the corporate embrace of the Establishment, dulling what little spark of intellect the listener might once have possessed with its hypnotic repetition of the message that everything was FINE.

Rock, on the other hand, confronted the burning issues of the day, and through the weight of public opinion, extinguished them. But where did you draw the line? SERGEANT PEPPER was rock, it was art. But *Lucy In The Sky With Diamonds*, for all John Lennon's coy references to drugs — and equally coy denials — was less than Pop, it was pap. And were *When I'm 64, Lovely Rita, Good Morning, Sergeant Pepper* itself, any better?

Iron Butterfly's *In-A-Gadda-Da-Vida*, that, too, was rock. But it made as much sense on AM Radio as it did on FM. And while Butterfly enthusiasts could argue all day that in breaching the Top 40, the band were striking a shattering blow against the empire, what was *In-A-*

Gadda-Da-Vida really, but another harmless pop narcotic, albeit a particularly overlong one, with no more social significance than the Ohio Express? Ellie and Howie, upstairs at Brill, might even have knocked out something similar five years before — but *In-a-gadda-da-doo-ron-ron* simply didn't sound too catchy back then. And even in 1967 — if rock really was going to change the world, it would have to do a lot better than that.

The whole concept of rock as a political force was born out of the Viet-Nam war, and the assorted Human Rights campaigns of the mid-to-late 1960's. It was, therefore, unquestionably held in the blood free hands of the Revolution. The Pop Groups, on the other hand, were the establishment's way of making people forget what was going on in the real world.

But who really sold the Underground? Jefferson Airplane signed to RCA, Janis Joplin to Columbia, the Doors to Elektra, the Dead to Warner Brothers. Suddenly, the war, and over fifty thousand American servicemen who were to die in a foreign land, became a commodity, packaged as neatly as love and peace and going to San Francisco with a flower in your hair.

The bands themselves were undoubtedly sincere in their motives, but to the major record companies who, at the end of the day, controlled the purse strings, they were simply filling a demand. The kids want protests, the record companies sold them protests. It was quite possibly the most callous marketing campaign ever launched, and so successful was it that most people weren't even aware how many of the labels involved were simply subsidiaries of vaster corporations who were equally bound up in the war effort itself. That, perhaps, was the ultimate irony, the war being financed by the very people who wanted it to stop!

The Pop groups, on the other hand, were firmly in the hands of the Independents. Buddah, Bell, Team, Calendar and Kirshner might have been allied, through distribution, to the major labels, but their interests were entirely self-serving.

Sure they manipulated the market, but they manipulated it for their own ends. It was still capitalism, but it was honest capitalism. When you bought a Fruitgums single it was a few cents more towards somebody's next limo. When you bought a Progressive album, God only knew where the money went. Bubblegum was formula music, but if only people had cared to look beyond the next chorus of whichever revolutionary chest beater they were chanting that day, they would have realized that in many cases the alternative was little better, and probably a lot worse. Serious rock music received all the attention, but it was the Bubblegum buyers who were the real revolutionaries. And when the revolution finally came, it wasn't Country Joe And The Fish who inspired it.

Simon says "up against the wall, mf's."

Discography:
Singles
- *Beg Borrow And Steal / Maybe* (Cameo 483, 1968)
- *Try It / Soul Struttin'* (Cameo 2001, 1968)

The Ohio Express

- *Yummy Yummy Yummy / ZigZag* (Buddah 38, 1968)
- *Down At Lulu's / She's Not Comin' Home* (Buddah 56, 1968)
- *Chewy Chewy / Firebird* (Buddah 70, 1968)
- *Sweeter Than Sugar / Boo Boo* (Buddah 92, 1969)
- *Mercy / Roll It Up* (Buddah 102, 1969)
- *Love = Love /* (Buddah 110, 1969)
- *Pinch Me (Baby, Convince Me) / Peanuts* (Buddah 117, 1969)
- *Sausalito / Make Love, Not War* (Buddah 129, 1969)
- *Cowboy Convention / The Race* (Buddah 147, 1969)
- *Love = Love / Peanuts* (Buddah 160, 1970)
- *Hot Dog / Ooh La La* (Super K 14, 1970)

Albums
- BEG BORROW AND STEAL (Cameo 20000, 1968)
- OHIO EXPRESS / YUMMY YUMMY YUMMY (Buddah 5018, 1968)
- CHEWY CHEWY (Buddah 5026, 1968)
- MERCY (Buddah 5037, 1969)
- VERY BEST OF (Buddah 5058, 1970)

~ 13 ~
The 1910 Fruitgum Company

1968: *Simon Says*

Like *Yummy Yummy Yummy*, like *Mony Mony*, the 1910 Fruitgum Company's *Simon Says* operated on the most basic level imaginable, a nursery rhyme standard set to the simplest of tunes, with the breeziest of lyrics. Indeed, Simon Says itself is a long-established playroom game in which the participants are given a variety of commands, and eliminated if they follow any not prefaced by the words "Simon Says." The song followed those rules to the letter.

Having wiped the floor with *Mony Mony* in American chart terms, *Simon Says* proceeded to do the same to competition everywhere else. Over five million copies were shifted, sold to parents wanting to give Junior a game to play, to teachers hoping to introduce First Graders to drama through a medium with which they were already familiar, and to pre-teens simply because they liked it.

The Fruitgums — whose name, incidentally, allegedly came from a gum wrapper discovered in the pocket of some antique clothes they were looking through — followed *Simon Says* with *1-2-3 Red Light*, in August, 1967, and by the end of the year, Kasenatz-Katz were all powerful. With seven Top 40 hits under their belts, and a production team which included Art Resnick, Joey Levine and Ritchie Cordell, their sound — the Sound of Super K — was, exactly as they had predicted it would be, no less recognizable than Spector's, and at this point in time, no less salable.

When they put together the Kasenatz-Katz Singing Orchestral Circus, a 46-strong aggregation drawn from the ranks of bands and producers alike, they sold out Carnegie Hall on the strength of their reputation alone. Kasenatz-Katz was a brand name at least as well known as the bands themselves. Like Wily E. Coyote and his eternal patronage of ACME Products, you didn't ask for the new Fruitgums single, you asked for the new Kasenatz-Katz. And when you went along to Carnegie Hall to see the Circus, you weren't going for J.C.W. Ratfink or the 1989 Marching Musical Zoo, you went to be part of the magic that was Super K.

The Circus was regarded by many as Super K's masterstroke, the ultimate culmination of their chosen art form. In fact, it was a plea for moderation. Kasenatz-Katz had made their way to the peak of their profession, but who cared? Kids bought their records, bought them in prodigious quantities. But kids didn't talk in hushed, reverent tones of the stunning production techniques, and the revolutionary use of echo, they simply knew the Sound of Super-K in the way their mothers knew which brand of washing powder to use.

Kasenatz-Katz wanted a little credibility, and the only way they could get it was by letting everybody else in on the joke. Thus Jerry And Jeff, Super K themselves, whose solitary single featured a pre-Dawn Tony Orlando on vocals; thus the Circus; thus the St. Louis Invisible Marching Band and Lieutenant Garcia's Magic Music Box (Dead-heads would have loved that one!); thus Captain Groovy And His Bubblegum Army (and the single of the same name); and thus, the Rock'n'Roll Dubble Bubble Trading Card Company of Philadelphia, 1941.

Their own Super K label sprang into being, employing the services not only of the proven Buddah stable, but also a host of its own "discoveries" — Buckwheat (not the Our Gang member, but a dubious sextet of the same name), the Shadows of Knight and Jerry and Jeff . . . yes, that Jerry and Jeff. The songs weren't hits, but they weren't expected to be. Rather, they were parodies, the Super K guys biting the sound which fed them, a slice of brilliant reverse psychology which insisted that the dumber we act, the more folks will like us. And the only thing wrong with that was, it didn't work.

Super K was still capable of some great music, though. *Quick Joey Small*, released under the name of the Circus, was a brilliantly constructed jailbreak song, one of the best of all time. The Shadows Of Knight's *Shake* was equally well-made, and prompted considerable comment from without, if only from people trying to work out what a mean lookin' bunch of garage critters like the Shads were doing making records with Kasenatz-Katz.

If they re-read the sleeve notes to the band's first (pre-Super K) album, though, they would have understood: "If you invited them over for dinner your parents would, at first, have you examined, or call the police, or run screaming to the neighbors. If your parents stayed around, they would find the Shadows are polite, quiet, considerate, and that they might even grow to like them." No brooding punk image here, the Shadows of Knight were good boys who only sounded like they'd strangle your granny as soon as look at her. In reality, they'd probably want to help you feed her, then stick around to help you clean the bubblegum off her dentures.

Discography:
Singles
- *Simon Says / Reflections From The Looking Glass* (Buddah 24, 1968)
- *May I Take A Giant Step / Poor Old Mr. Jensen* (Buddah 39, 1968)
- *1, 2, 3 Red Light / Sticky Sticky* (Buddah 54, 1968)
- *Goody Goody Gumdrops / Candy Kisses* (Buddah 71, 1968)
- *Indian Giver / Pow Wow* (Buddah 91, 1969)
- *Special Delivery / No Good Annie* (Buddah 114, 1969)
- *The Train / Huff Puff* (Buddah 130, 1970)
- *When We Get Married / Baby Bret* (Buddah 146, 1970)
- *Go Away / The Track* (Super K 15, 1968)
- *Lawdy, Lawdy / The Clock* (Attack 10293, 1970)
Albums
- SIMON SAYS (Buddah 5010, 1968)
- 1, 2, 3 RED LIGHT (Buddah 5022, 1968)
- GOODY GOODY GUMDROPS (Buddah 5027, 1968)
- INDIAN GIVER (Buddah 5036, 1969)
- HARD RIDE (Buddah 5043, 1969)
- THE JUICIEST FRUITGUM (Buddah 5057, 1970)

~ 14 ~
Tommy Roe

1969: *Dizzy*

By 1969, Kasenatz Katz ruled the American pop roost, no question. Tommy James' continued domination of the Top 40 was immaterial, the Shondells having so beautifully transcended the Bubblegum genre that they were almost respectable; while the handful of other contenders — the Cowsills included — simply didn't have what it took to stick around long.

Allentown cuties Jay And The Techniques might have constituted a threat had their promotion been as good as their lyrics ("Apple, Peaches, Pumpkin Pie, You were young and so was I" is a great line whichever way you look at it.) Fun And Games came close with *The Grooviest Girl In The World* — hip language and a bouncy little beat! — but foundered in the follow-up stakes. And though England's Yardbirds were jolted out of their primeval Metal meanderings and put to task by producer Micky Most's insistence that they now sing Top 40 material — *Ha Ha Said The Clown*, *Ten Little Indians* — the band broke up before they could do too much damage.

And then there was Tommy Roe, an early 60's balladeer who had been bubbling around the pop scene for years. His first hit, 1962's *Sheila*, made No. 1, and though a few follow-ups failed, *Everybody* (1963), *Sweet Pea* and *Hooray For Hazel* (both 1966) at least kept up the veneer of a Top 10 presence.

1969, however, brought a comeback which few could have predicted, opening with a sensational No. 1, the giddying *Dizzy*, and then taking the very concept of bubblegum to whole new heights with the release of *Jam Up Jelly Tight*, a No. 8 in late 1969, and possibly the rudest song ever to make it that far past the censors. Possibly.

"Jam up jelly tight, you look a little naughty, but you're so polite, Jam up jelly tight, you won't say you will but there's a chance you might." There was a suggestiveness to such lyrics which turned faces as red as, indeed, jam. This was perhaps the Industry's response to the dirty versions of *Simon Says* which percolated among the burgeoning adolescents in the school yard — "Simon Says 'Show me your thingy'," that kind of thing.

And it was true, Kasenatz-Katz themselves had already intimated that the innocence with which they imbibed their best work was only as chaste as the people who listened to it — *Yummy Yummy Yummy*, for instance, warned, "I love you such a sweet thing, good enough to eat thing, and that's just what I'm gonna do." *Jam Up Jelly Tight* was simply the next step down the road. But if there were any depths of depravity to be plumbed, *Cinnamon* by Derek — Johnny Cymbal of the five year old *Mr. Bass Man* fame — was the song to plumb them.

Tommy Roe

Of course, it was impossible to actually be offended by the song, even when Derek insisted that Cinnamon "open up" because he "wanted more." At worst it was naive foreplay, nothing more than that. It was never going to corrupt anyone. But that's not to say that Bubblegum was to remain the asexual, faceless beastling which Kasenatz-Katz had created, and the likes of Derek and Tommy Roe could only snipe at from afar.

If there was any flaw in the Super K game plan, it was that while they had sewn up the sing-along, dance-along market, they had made no provision whatsoever for their audience's other prime fixation — love. Sure they sang about it, but they did so in a most impersonal way. You could like the 1910 Fruitgum Company, you could even look at their pictures on the record sleeve and think they were cute. But unless you could get to know them intimately, you could never fall in love with them. And that, as the new decade grew ever closer, was a problem which a number of people would be coming to grips with.

But before that, there was one final, crowning piece of nonsense to dispense with.

Discography:
Singles
  ° *Caveman* / *I Got A Girl* (Judd 1018, 1960)
  ° *Sheila* / *Pretty Girl* (Judd 1022, 1961)
  ° *Sheila* / *Save Your Kisses* (ABC 10329, 1962)
  ° *Susie Darlin'* / *Piddle-de-pat* (ABC 10362, 1962)
  ° *Town Crier* / *Rainbow* (ABC 10379, 1962)
  ° *Don't Cry Donna* / *Gonna Take A Chance* (ABC 10389, 1963)
  ° *The Folk Singer* / *Count On Me* (ABC 10423, 1963)
  ° *Kiss And Run* / *What Makes The Blues* (ABC 10454, 1963)
  ° *Everybody* / *Sorry I'm Late, Lisa* (ABC 10478, 1963)
  ° *Come On* / *There'll Be Better Years* (ABC 10515, 1964)
  ° *Carol* / *Be A Good Little Girl* (ABC 10543, 1964)
  ° *Dance With Me Henry* / *Wild Water Skiing Weekend* (ABC 10555, 1964)
  ° *Oh So Right* / *I Think I Love You* (ABC 10579, 1964)
  ° *Diane From Manchester Square* / *Love Me* (ABC 10623, 1965)
  ° *Fourteen Pairs Of Shoes* / *Combo Music* (ABC 10665, 1965)
  ° *I'm A Rambler* / *Gunfighter* (ABC 10696, 1965)
  ° *I Keep Remembering* / *Wish You Didn't Have To Go* (ABC 10706, 1967)
  ° *Everytime A Bluebird Cries* / *Doesn't Anybody Know* (ABC 10738, 1965)
  ° *Sweet Pea* / *Much More Love* (ABC 10762, 1966)
  ° *Hooray For Hazel* / *Need Your Love* (ABC 10852, 1966)
  ° *It's Now Winter's Day* / *Kick Me Charlie* (ABC 10888, 1966)
  ° *Singing Along With Me* / *Nighttime* (ABC 10908, 1967)
  ° *Sweet Sounds* / *Moon Talk* (ABC 10933, 1967)
  ° *Little Miss Sunshine* / *The You I Need* (ABC 10945, 1967)
  ° *Melancholy Wood* / *Paisley Dreams* (ABC 10989, 1967)
  ° *Dottie I Like It* / *Soft Words* (ABC 11039, 1968)
  ° *Oldies But Goldies* / *Sugar Cane* (ABC 11076, 1968)
  ° *Gotta Keep Rolling Along* / *Gonna Hurt Me* (ABC 11140, 1968)
  ° *Dizzy* / *The You I Need* (ABC 11164, 1969)

- *Heather Honey / Money Is My Pay* (ABC 11211, 1969)
- *Jack And Jill / Tiptoe Tina* (ABC 11229, 1969)
- *Jam Up Jelly Tight / Moon Talk* (ABC 11247, 1969)
- *Stir It Up And Serve It / Firefly* (ABC 11258, 1970)
- *Pearl / A Dollar's Worth Of Pennies* (ABC 11266, 1970)
- *We Can Make Music / Gotta Keep Rollin' Along* (ABC11273, 1970)
- *Brush A Little Sunshine / King Of Fools* (ABC 11281, 1970)
- *Miss Goodie-Two Shoes / Traffic Jam* (ABC 11287, 1970)
- *Pistol Legged Mama / King Of Fools* (ABC 11293, 1971)
- *Stagger Lee / Back Streets & Alleys* (ABC 11307, 1971)
- *Mean Little Woman / Rosalie* (MGM 7001, 1972)
- *Chewin' On Sugarcane / Sarah My Love* (MGM 7008, 1972)
- *Working Class Hero / Sun In My Eyes* (MGM 7013, 1973)

Albums
- SHEILA (ABC 423, 1962)
- TOMMY ROE (ABC 432, 1962)
- SOMETHING FOR EVERYBODY (ABC 467, 1964)
- SWEET PEA / HOORAY FOR HAZEL (ABC 575, 1966)
- IT'S NOW WINTER'S DAY (ABC 594, 1967)
- PHANTASY (ABC 610, 1967)
- DIZZY (ABC 683, 1969)
- 12 IN A ROE — A COLLECTION ... (ABC 700, 1969)
- WE CAN MAKE MUSIC (ABC 714, 1970)
- BEGINNINGS (ABC 732, 1971)
- 16 GREATEST HITS (ABC 762, 1972)

~ 15 ~
The Archies

1969: *Sugar Sugar*

The Archies were the direct descendants of The Monkees — totally prefabricated, totally innocent, and totally phony. Archie loved Betty, Reggie loved Veronica, drummer Jughead loved Hot Dog the dog and the old jalopy that got him from Riverdale High to Pop's Choklit Shoppe. There was no sex, although one of the boys might peck a girl on the cheek at the end of the day. There was no violence, even though Archie himself sounded pretty mean when he warned Reggie "Don't touch my guitar," there were no drugs and, of course, there were no musicians.

But there was a lot of fun, good, clean fun and a lot of music, good, clean music. Creator Don Kirshner had learned the hard way, after all — even puppets have feelings sometimes. The Archies, then, took the idea of a manufactured pop group to its most logical extreme. They were a cartoon.

Don Kirshner's Archie Show was premiered on a Saturday morning, traditional TV cartoon time, September 14, 1968, and would ultimately run for eight seasons. Pre-release hype had already cited The Archies as Kirshner's answer to The Monkees, which in itself was a rather cruel gibe. But neither Kirshner nor the network, CBS, actually wanted to compete with the Prefab Four. They wanted more than that — they wanted to replace them. The Monkees was off the air when The Archies came into being, no one knew if there would even be another series. But there was still an audience out there, the eight to twelve year olds whose lives would suddenly be that little bit emptier without Davy, Micky, Pete and Mike to fill the void.

And while The Archies could never offer the romantic involvement which The Monkees had promised, everything else about them was perfect. Their adventures, usually involving straight-laced figures of authority who wanted to stop them playing their music or going down to Pop's, were adventures everyone could identify with. And even more than The Monkees, The Archies played music you didn't even need to learn the lyrics to — it seemed as though you knew them already.

In November, the Archies' first single, *Bang-Shang-A-Lang*, taken from their first ever show, pierced the lower reaches of the Top Thirty with little more exposure than it received from The Archie Show itself. Neither was it a particularly memorable song, although when you did hear it, it was difficult to believe you'd ever get it out of your head again.

Not even Kirshner and The Archie Show producer Jeff Barry would have claimed it to be among their most exciting compositions, but there again, it wasn't meant to be. *Bang-Shang-A-Lang* was a tentative toe in the water, a cheap one shot designed to test the malleability of the market. Several years previous, Barry and partner Andy Kim had handed Kirshner a song called *Sugar Sugar*, which they thought might be suitable for the Monkees. Kirshner thought so too, but the Monkees, then at the height of their musical rebelliousness, had laughed it out of sight.

Kirshner kept his faith, however, and now, having reassessed its potential with a dry run, he was ready to commit his ace to the hole. Nine months, and one ill-conceived follow-up flop, *Feelin' So Good (S.K.O.O.B.Y.-D.O.O.),"* later, *Bang-Shang-A-Lang* was finally given a worthy successor — and one which topped the chart on both sides of the Atlantic, four weeks in America, eight in Great Britain.

It was a curious juxtaposition. The second season (now retitled The Archies' Comedy Hour) was still to get underway, but *Sugar Sugar* topped the US listings, and did so in the very same week as the anti-Establishment dream of "returning to the garden" appeared poised for fulfillment.

While half a million kids camped out in a field in the Catskills, the wail of Woodstock was an insignificant drone when compared to the sound blasting out of transistor radios everywhere else in the country — Ron Dante (who later led the Cufflinks to success with the equally icky *Tracy*) and Toni Wine (co-writer of The Mindbenders' *Groovy Kind Of Love* and later, an uncredited member of Dawn) trilling out lyrics which still send a shiver up the spine.

The Archies never recovered from their success. The show, at its peak, was beaming into even more homes than The Monkees had invaded, with a space-age spin-off, Josie And The Pussycats, cleaning up any flotsam the frontal assault may have missed.

But the Archies themselves were to enjoy just two further hits; *Jingle Jangle*, an infuriating powerhouse straight out of some TV ad man's wildest dream as sung by Betty and Veronica, and *Who's Your Baby*, a song which, ridiculous as it may sound, suffered from exactly the same terminal malaise as had afflicted The Monkees. The Archies wanted to make meaningful records!

Kirshner retaliated by not letting them make any records at all. The 1970 season, now retitled The Archies' TV Funnies, featured no music whatsoever; instead Kirshner returned his allegiance to real people. He reunited Neil Sedaka with old-time partner Howie Greenfield, paving the way for Sedaka's own sugar coated comeback of the early 1970's. He tried piecing together a new Unknowns Supergroup, Tomorrow, starring a fresh-faced Australian singer named Olivia Newton John, and then moved directly into television in his own right, presenting Don Kirshner's Rock Concert, one of the most successful live music programs of the new decade.

But behind him he left a fad run riot, a video boom which gave us everything from singing insects (The Bugaloos) and boogying bears (The Sugar Bears) to Britain's musical mice-alike (The Wombles), and then reached back into the Beatles' murkiest, *Yellow Submarine*, past to translate the latest product of the Motown hit machine, the Jackson Five, to the same animated medium.

Discography:
Singles
- *Bang Shang-A-Lang / Truck Driver* (Calendar 1006, 1968)
- *Feelin' So Good / Love Light* (Calendar 1007, 1968)
- *Sugar Sugar / Melody Hill* (Calendar 1008, 1969)
- *Sunshine / Over & Over* (Calendar 1009, 1969)
- *Jingle Jangle / Justine* (Kirshner 5002, 1969)
- *Who's Your Baby / Senorita Rita* (Kirshner 5003, 1970)
- *Together We Two / Everything's Alright* (Kirshner 5009, 1971)
- *This Is Love / Throw A Little Love My Way* (Kirshner 5011, 1971)
- *Summer Prayer For Peace / Maybe I'm Wrong* (Kirshner 5014, 1971)
- *Hold Onto Loving / Love Is Living With You* (Kirshner 5018, 1971)

○ *Strangers In The Morning* / *Plumb Crazy* (Kirshner 5021, 1972)

Flexi-Discs

Cardboard discs pressed into the back of the cereal packets. At least two different picture designs of which were available.

○ *Bang Shang-A-Lang* (Post Cereal no catalog #, 1969)
○ *Hide And Seek* (Post Cereal no catalog #, 1969)
○ *Love Light* (Post Cereal no catalog #, 1969)
○ *Feelin' So Good* (Post Cereal no catalog #, 1969)
○ *Boys And Girls* (Post Cereal no catalog #, 1969)
○ *Hide And Seek* (Post Cereal no catalog #, 1969)
○ *Sugar Sugar* (Post Cereal no catalog #, 1969)
○ *Archies' Party* (Post Cereal no catalog #, 1969)
○ *Jingle Jangle* (Post Cereal no catalog #, 1969)
○ *You Know I Love You* (Post Cereal no catalog #, 1969)
○ *Nursery Rhyme* (Post Cereal no catalog #, 1969)
○ *Catchin' Up On Fun* (Post Cereal no catalog #, 1969)
○ *Everything's Archie* (Post Cereal no catalog #, 1969)
○ *You Make Me Wanna Dance* (Post Cereal no catalog #, 1969)

Albums

○ THE ARCHIES (Calendar 101, 1968)
○ EVERYTHING'S ARCHIE (Calendar 103, 1969) (reissued as "Sugar Sugar", 1970)
○ JINGLE JANGLE (Kirshner 105, 1970)
○ SUNSHINE (Kirshner 107, 1970)
○ GREATEST HITS (Kirshner 109, 1970)
○ THIS IS LOVE (Kirshner 110, 1971)
○ THE BEST OF THE ARCHIES (Kirshner 1250, 1971)

~ 16 ~
The Jackson Five

1969: *I Want You Back*

Motown was first alerted to the Five by Gladys Knight, although it was Diana Ross who was ultimately to become the family's sponsor. The Five were, in reality, nine; the stage performers Michael, Tito, Jermaine, Jackie and Marlon; a younger brother, Randy, who was already being groomed to step into Michael's pre-pubescent shoes the moment the older boy's voice started to break; cousins Ronnie Ransom and Johnny Jackson, the only real musicians in sight; and papa Joe Jackson, an ex-R&B guitarist who started pushing his brood into show biz the moment they opened their eyes.

With Michael, a born mimic, leading the way with his note-perfect James Brown routines, the family would pile into a van and hit clubs as far apart as New York and Phoenix, and by the time la Belle Knight came across them, the troupe had already been sighted by Sam Moore, of Sam & Dave and Stax Records fame.

But it was Berry Gordy, Knight's boss at Motown, who swooped first, intuitively aware of the family's inevitable stardom, instinctively knowing that, just as the Supremes' name had once been powerful enough to package bread, so the Jacksons were just so hale and wholesome, cute and cuddly, that Middle America would be powerless to resist.

Black Militancy was at its peak, but in the eyes of the marketing boys, the Jackson Five were totally divorced from all that. And when ABC gifted Diana Ross with her own networked special, it was her little guests who stole the show, especially Michael. In one segment he was Frank Sinatra, in another he whirled like a dervish, and in all, he won the hearts of the watching millions.

In December, 1969, the glorious *I Want You Back* gave the family its first hit single, and one of the finest Motown singles ever. One of the most furiously aped as well: a slab of effervescent joy, *I Want You Back* opened the floodgates for a succession of sound-alike smashes — from everyone, it seemed, bar the Jacksons themselves.

ABC followed *I Want You Back* to the top of the chart in the new year, and by the end of 1970 the Five had notched up two more number ones, a top-rated television special of their own, and a Saturday morning cartoon series. And though the latter was little more than a Hard Day's Animated Monkee Bizness, with the Five having nothing more to do with it than standing still long enough for the artists to come up with passable likenesses, and supplying a soundtrack carefully arranged to give maximum exposure to whatever their latest release might be, still the show repaid them in full.

In a way that the Archies and the Monkees (and the Cowsills) never had, the Jackson Five were to prove all powerful. The teen press adored them and the serious press respected them. Blithely, they would cover a Bobby Day song with one single, a Jackson Browne number with another, assimilating the best parts of each into an easily recognizable Jackson sound which carried the Motown stable into the Seventies all but single-handedly, and made Michael a superstar with room to spare. Just as they had with the youthful Stevie Wonder, Motown pushed Michael into every arena they could fit him into, Unlike "Little" Stevie Wonder, who was brindling at such handling long before he finally rebelled, Michael appeared to love every minute of it.

Yet the acclaim he and his brothers were to receive was to be tempered throughout by the industry's recollection of another precocious black juvenile, fifteen years previous.

The Jackson Five

Just like Michael and his brothers, Frankie Lyman, too, had scythed through the boundaries of color and creed and won the hearts of black and white audiences alike. He was just 13 when he landed a Top 10 smash with the anthemic *Why Do Fools Fall In Love*, and kicked a whole teen industry into life. No less than Presley before him (and Michael Jackson after), little Frankie dominated the fan mags and should have been set up for life. Instead, when things turned sour and the hits stopped sticking, he sank like a stone. He wound up dead aged just 25.

Neither Motown nor Ma and Pa Jackson could ever prepare their own brood for the so callously fickle attentions of the outside world. But they could close ranks to protect their charges from its more damaging manifestations, and it was this, as much as any level-headedness on the part of the band members themselves, which was to keep the Jackson Five on a level footing at all stages of their career. Indeed, the whole "Is Jacko Wacko?" scam so beloved by the western world's tabloid press in the post-THRILLER 80's (and brilliantly parodied in Michael's *Leave Me Alone* video) was derived purely from the closeted world in which Michael, in particular, was to grow up, and in which he is still said to live.

Even at the age of 11 or 12, Michael was a phenomenal talent. He was the star of the family group; the star, in fact, of American youth, and any number of outside concerns would have paid any amount of money to have got their hands on him. So, when they found out that they couldn't, they just took that money elsewhere, and set about building their own little Michaels instead.

Discography:
Singles
- *Big Boy / You've Changed* (Steeltown 681, 1968)
- *You Don't Have To Be Over 21 / Some Girls Want Me For Their Love* (Steeltown 684, 1968)
- *I Want You Back / Who's Loving You* (Motown 1157, 1970)
- *ABC / The Young Folks* (Motown 1163, 1970)
- *The Love You Save / I Found That Girl* (Motown 1166, 1970)
- *I'll Be There / One More Chance* (Motown 1171, 1970)
- *Santa Claus Is Coming To Town / Christmas Won't Be The Same* (Motown 1174, 1971)
- *Mama's Pearl / Darling Dear* (Motown 1177, 1971)
- *Never Can Say Goodbye / She's Good* (Motown 1179, 1971)
- *Maybe Tomorrow / I Will Find A Way* (Motown 1186, 1971)
- *Sugar Daddy / I'm So Happy* (Motown 1194, 1972)
- *Little Bitty Pretty One / If I Have To Move A Mountain* (Motown 1199, 1972)
- *Lookin' Through The Windows / Love Song* (Motown 1205, 1972)
- *Corner Of The Sky / To Know* (Motown 1214, 1972)
- *Hallelujah Day / You Make Me What I Am* (Motown 1224, 1973)

Albums
- DIANA ROSS PRESENTS (Motown 700, 1969)
- ABC (Motown 709, 1970)
- CHRISTMAS ALBUM (Motown 713, 1970)

- THIRD ALBUM (Motown 718, 1970)
- MAYBE TOMORROW (Motown 735, 1971)
- GREATEST HITS (Motown 741, 1971)
- GOIN' BACK TO INDIANA (Motown 742, 1971)
- LOOKIN' THROUGH THE WINDOWS (Motown 750, 1972)
- SKYWRITER (Motown 761, 1973)
- GET IT TOGETHER (Motown 783, 1973)

JACKIE JACKSON
Albums
- JACKIE JACKSON (Motown 785, 1973)

JERMAINE JACKSON
Singles
- *That's How Love Goes / I Lost My Love In The Big City* (Motown 1201, 1972)
- *Daddy's Home / Take Me In Your Arms* (Motown 1216, 1972)
- *Does Your Mama Know About Me / You're In Good Hands* (Motown 1244, 1973)

Albums
- JERMAINE (Motown 752, 1973)
- COME INTO MY LIFE (Motown 775, 1973)

MICHAEL JACKSON
Singles
- *Got To Be There / Maria* (Motown 1191, 1972)
- *Rockin' Robin / Love Is Here* (Motown 1197, 1972)
- *I Wanna Be Where You Are / We've Got A Good Thing Going* (Motown 1202, 1972)
- *Ben / You Can Cry On My Shoulder* (Motown 1207, 1972)
- *With A Child's Heart / Morning Glow* (Motown 1218, 1973)

Albums
- GOT TO BE THERE (Motown 747, 1972)
- BEN (Motown 755, 1972)
- MUSIC AND ME (Motown 767, 1973)
- THE BEST OF MICHAEL JACKSON (Motown 851, 1975)

~ 17 ~
The Pipkins

1970: *Gimme Dat Ding*

At the outset of the 70's, British bubblegum meant three things: the Pipkins, Hotlegs and the Sweet. The first, of course, was nothing more than another stepping stone in the career of Tony Burroughs, the self-styled King of anonymous British session singers. The second was a trio of Manchester session men who were friends with Herman's Hermits. And the third was a four piece combo which grew from the wreckage of sundry 60's progressive bands, before falling under the spell of glam rock kingpins Nicky Chinn and Mike Chapman, and a sensational *Sugar Sugar* sound-alike called *Funny Funny*.

Between them, the two summed up everything that the genre could demand from its progenitors. And while the Sweet would go on to enjoy a remarkable, and remarkably long career, the Pipkins so admirably filled all the criteria of true pop that they should be enrolled in the Ephemeral Hall Of Fame without delay. For they were, and remain, perfect.

The Pipkins developed out of Burrough's career with the likes of Edison Lighthouse, Brotherhood Of Man and White Plains, purveyors of so many magical pop lite moments that today, entire compilation albums are created from Burrough's back pages. In early 1970, however, he was appearing alongside songwriter Roger Greenaway on the childrens' TV show Oliver And The Overworld, and creating songs . . . which children would like. Of course.

The almost frighteningly contagious *Gimme Dat Ding* — originally titled *Gimme That Click* — was a conversation between a pianola and a broken metronome, and was just so idiosyncratic that attempts to follow it with an entire album's worth of similar sounds failed dismally. While it lasted though, success was hot. The Pipkins became TV superstars, in their baggy pants and pantomime hats. *Gimme Dat Ding* was a hit throughout the broken-English speaking world. And in the US, it was reissued some years later back to back with Hotlegs' *Neanderthal Man*, to present the very best of primal British bubblegum on one single!

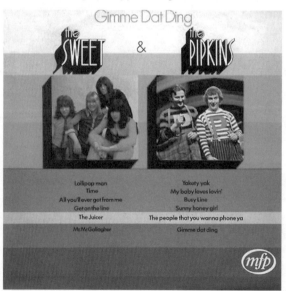

Discography:
Singles
- ○ *Gimme Dat Ding / To Love You* (Capitol 2819, 1970)
- ○ *Yakkety Yak / Sugar And Spice* (Capitol 2874, 1970)

Albums
- ○ THE PIPKINS (Capitol 483, 1970)

~ 18 ~
Hotlegs

1970: *Neanderthal Man*

Kasenatz-Katz's own attempts to break into television were, sadly, doomed to failure. Captain Groovy's Bubblegum Show was intended to queer The Archies' pitch by introducing cartoon replicas of the 1910 Fruitgum Company, Crazy Elephant and The Ohio Express alongside an array of custom built adventurers. But it never got off the ground, a fate which also befell a projected documentary, We All Got High On Bubblegum.

So now the duo turned their attention towards a very different end of the market entirely and promptly subverted it to their own ends with the pounding might of Crazy Elephant, the band who the duo maintained were discovered in a Welsh coal mine.

Created by Ritchie Cordell and Joey Levine, Crazy Elephant's *Gimme Gimme Good Loving* had very little in common with Kasenatz-Katz, but an awful lot to do with the heavy rock boom now beginning to glower over the horizon. Above a thundering rhythm, a piping organ and stone chisel guitars, the Crazy Elephant — featuring Bob Avery from the Music Explosion and Fruitgum Ralph Cohen's brother Kenny — chanted their way into every hit parade in the west. And thoughts turned towards a follow-up.

Late in 1969, Kasenatz-Katz approached English songsmith Graham Gouldman with the offer of working for them. Throughout the decade, Gouldman had established himself as one of his homeland's foremost writers — maybe not as consistent as the likes of Lennon / McCartney, Jagger / Richard and Ray Davies, but capable of running rings around any of them when he really set his mind to it.

The Yardbirds' *For Your Love*, Wayne Fontana's *Pamela Pamela*, Jeff Beck's *Tallyman*, Herman's *No Milk Today* and the Hollies' intoxicatingly sublime *Bus Stop* were the best of his efforts, but even the worst was worth a few minutes of anyone's attention. Gouldman had also tried breaking into the bubblegum market, first via the Graham Gouldman Orchestra's lightweight versions of his own greatest hits, then through an ill-fated liaison with Giorgio Gomelsky's short-lived Marmalade label. More recently, he had been concentrating on trying to salvage one-time chart heroes the Mindbenders, and investing in his own Strawberry Studios recording plant with fellow 'bender, Eric Stewart.

Kasenatz-Katz's offer, and the advance it promised, came just at the right time — "just as I was getting married." It gave Kasenatz-Katz publishing and performing rights to anything Gouldman wrote while in their employ, and guaranteed them unlimited studio time at the newly built Strawberry. But it also gave Gouldman a lot of much needed money.

It was a windfall he and Stewart simply couldn't turn down, although Gouldman admits that when it came to persuading anybody else to work with him, it was a different matter entirely. Kevin Godley and Lol Creme, two dilettante art students whom Gouldman and Stewart had known since childhood (and who had also been involved with the Marmalade label in the guise of Frabjoy & The Runcible Spoon, a psychedelic Simon & Garfunkel), were particularly mortified at the prospect: "they always had very high ambitions," Gouldman reflected, "they believed in what they were doing, and were appalled that I should even suggest such a thing. I really had to work hard at persuading them to do it, and even then it was only the money which convinced them. We were very well paid for churning that stuff out."

Summoned to New York, Gouldman slipped straight into the hit factory routine. "The whole thing was incredible, and it's difficult to believe I ever did it, although I realize now just how good it was for me. Over a period of one year I wrote, and saw recorded, about twenty songs, which was a very high output for me."

Among his more accomplished efforts during this period were *Susan's Tuba*, which sold over two million copies in France for fellow Manchester lad Freddie Garrity and his Dreamers; the Ohio Express' *Sausalito* and *Tampa, Florida*; and *Have You Ever Been To Georgia*, a song which so utterly transcended its intended bubblegum catchment area that it gave balladeer Tony Christie — who shared Gouldman's management company — a worldwide hit.

In personal terms, however, the most important of all the Kasenatz-Katz / Strawberry songs was *There Ain't No Umbopo*, written by Godley and Creme and released under the Crazy Elephant brand name. (According to Creme, "There were singles coming out by us under all manner of different names. It was impossible to keep track of them all!")

A copy found its way to Neil Sedaka, who promptly flipped. He demanded an instant introduction to the minds behind the song, and with manager Don Kirshner anxious only to get the former teenage idol's career back on the tracks, he was dispatched across to Manchester to set the ball rolling. Sedaka's multi-million selling SOLITAIRE album, recorded at Strawberry with the house team in full attendance, was the result. That, and another brick in the wall of experience which would soon become 10cc, perhaps the single most innovative British band of the past two decades.

Indeed, no sooner had they finished work on *Umbopo*, and Gouldman returned to New York, than the remainder of the team found themselves staring another monster in the face, simply because a passing A&R man caught them testing the drum sound in the studio one day, and thought he smelled a smash hit. He thought right.

Stewart recalls, "Dick Leahy, from Phillips, came in and he said, 'What the hell's that you're playing?' I said, 'It's a studio experiment; a percussive experiment.' He says, 'It sounds like a hit record to me . . .' and 'Can we release it?' And we said, 'Yeh, okay. What should we call it?' And we had no name for the group, of course. But we had a girl at the studio . . . Kathy Gill, I think her name was, yeh . . . who had very, very nice legs and she used to wear these incredible hot pants. Green, leather hot pants. So we called the group, ah, Hotlegs."

Restructured and released just in time for the summer silly season, *Neanderthal Man* reached No. 22 in the US, No. 2 in Britain, No. 1 in Italy, and ultimately sold over two million worldwide. The record was enormous: the Idle Race, heading towards the end of their brief but glorious career, wrested one final hit from the jaws of oblivion when they covered the song for German and Argentine consumption; Elton John, eking out a pre-fame career as a jobbing sessioneer, recorded his own distinctive version for a budget priced collection of sound-alike hits. No matter where you went that summer, the crazed beat of *Neanderthal Man* would be pounding out.

But with success came a sting. While Hotlegs went on to tour with the Moody Blues, and record an album of almost exclusively — and exquisitely — dissimilar songs, still most folk simply filed them alongside the Pipkins, and wrote them off entirely. The album died, two follow-up singles sank, and within six months, Godley, Creme and Stewart were back on the pop production line, cutting singles with such giants of music as Manchester City soccer team, and a local cricket side.

In historical terms, the ultimate failure of Hotlegs simply caused Godley, Creme and Stewart to place their plans for a serious band on hold, at least until the pure pop sensibilities of Gouldman returned to England. In more general terms, however, it can be regarded as more than ironic that no sooner had Britain finally cracked the US bubblegum market, with the manufactured joys of the Pipkins and Hotlegs, than the pendulum swung once again, and suddenly people didn't want cartoon pop any more. The market had returned to Real People for its kicks, and with the Jackson Five having already wrapped up the role of founding fathers, it was a two way fight for God-parenthood. In the white corner, from Los Angeles, California, David Cassidy and the Partridge family; and in the whiter-than-white corner, all the way from Utah, the Osmond Brothers.

Discography:
Singles
  ○ *Neanderthal Man* / *You Didn't Like It* (Capitol 2886, 1970)
  ○ *How Many More Times* / *Run Baby Run* (Capitol 3043, 1971)
Albums
  ○ THINKS: SCHOOL STINKS (Capitol 587, 1970)

~ 19 ~
The Partridge Family

1970: *I Think I Love You*

In September, 1970, Screen Gems / Columbia launched The Partridge Family, a 30 minute sit-com concerning a singing, dancing, one parent family growing up in middle class America. It was based, very loosely indeed, on the lives of the Cowsills, but it was aimed at a considerably older audience than either its role models or, bearing in mind the undoubted influence of the Jacksons, its contemporaries. Whereas the Jacksons' cartoon show went out on Saturday mornings, The Partridge Family had its own peak time evening slot, smack in the middle of Family Viewing Hour.

Similarly, while both the Jacksons and later, the Osmonds, took for their focal point the youngest member of the crew, The Partridge Family revolved around the growing pains of the painfully good-looking, and decidedly post-adolescent, Keith Partridge — the then unknown David Cassidy. And with a remarkable twist, to which Cassidy at least was not party, the son of Broadway stars Jack Cassidy and Evelyn Ward was to be partnered in the series' star billing by his real-life stepmother, Shirley Jones.

It was her performance as the long suffering mother trying to keep the kids on an even keel which lent the show its most powerful images. It was her relationship with "son" "Keith" which provided many of the show's most pertinent sparks. She, too, was an accomplished player. David, for all his thespian ambition and heritage, had thus far developed only an endearing self-consciousness, while his screen sister Laurie — Susan Dey — was for the most part required to do nothing more than look pretty, represent the spirit of socially conscious youth, and pour scorn on David's crasser on-screen antics.

Of the three younger members of the cast, Danny — Danny Bonaduce, who grew to become a Philadelphia radio jock with an occasionally less than wholesome capacity for making tabloid headlines — wavered between an underaged prototype for the Michael J Fox role in Family Ties, and a precocious Beaver Cleaver; Tracy — Suzanne Crough — seemed to play less of a part in the action with every passing show, and Chris — Jeremy Gelbawks and later Brian Forster — for the most part simply stood around twiddling his thumbs and looking totally bewildered by everything.

The "kids" were largely irrelevant, anyway. Throughout its three year run, The Partridge Family profited immeasurably from its intended older adolescent catchment area, both in terms of viewing figures, and with regard to what the writers could get away with. Some surprisingly mature — or at least, innovative — story lines were introduced; Danny masquerading as a Jew so that he might date the daughter of a local Rabbi; Keith using a problem page edited by Laurie to win an introduction to a new girl in the neighborhood;

Laurie entering the Homecoming Queen competition so that she might use her acceptance speech as the platform for her feminist views. "In" jokes, too, proliferated. A show which revolves around Laurie's disdain of Keith as the idol of every girl in America closes with the Family performing before an audience whose average age has to be in the upper 40's. In another, the family dissuade Keith from pursuing a career in classical music by convincing him that his own songs are valid enough, then close by performing a Hermans' Hermits' cover. Sophisticated AND self-deprecating? Television had never known anything like it.

The Partridge Family had been on the air little more than a month before the family scored their first number one, and once again with their choice of material, and the manner in which they delivered it, *I Think I Love You* indicated just how much more sophisticated a market they were aiming to tap.

The first signs that the Family was about to explode into something far greater came when the teenybop magazines suddenly swooped upon Cassidy as the logical successor to Bobby Sherman, a pasty-faced youth who had set a million hearts a-flutter as co-star of Here Comes the Brides, and host of Shindig, and who was now finally reaping the rewards of a recording career which dated back to 1964.

It was plain what the attraction was. Cassidy was, first and foremost, exceedingly pretty, but reassuringly so. Lee Black Childers, a photographer at 16 Magazine around this time remembers most of his assignments involved "Standing 'em up against a wall, making sure their cigarettes didn't show and rearranging the bulge in their trousers so it wouldn't scare the eight year olds."

David Cassidy posed no such problems. When he confessed he still suffered from acne, he won a million soulmates overnight, fragile young things for whom adolescence was a constant battle against disfiguring pimples. He wore contact lenses, he worried about being too short, and he wore built-up shoes. All this was grist to the mill — at last, a star with faults!

Simply by virtue of the competition, David Cassidy was always regarded with a little more sympathy than either the Jacksons or the simultaneously blossoming Osmonds. For a start, he was hopelessly outnumbered, but more importantly, he never seemed to take his role as an "idol" too seriously.

On stage he would pepper his repertoire with material by artists he respected as musicians and writers, not because they wrote simple, sing-along melodies. Offstage, he viewed the maelstrom in which he was caught with an amused, almost bemused, attachment. When a Dutch radio interviewer asked him how he would go about kissing a girl, Cassidy replied, "First take a rope . . ." A decade later, older and wiser, he answered the same question, "First get a lawyer . . ."

Yet at the same time, he was occasionally persuaded to go along with the most ridiculous publicity stunts, not the least of which involved living on a boat moored in the middle of the River Thames during one of his London visits. "We were fishing them out of the water all week," a local policeman said of the fans.

Perhaps more than any other teen idol, Cassidy's career was a constant battle between his own love of privacy and his advisors' love of publicity. In an interview with Rolling Stone in 1972, he spoke quite openly about drink, drugs and sex. Weeks later he was denying it and claiming he'd been misquoted, only to repeat highlights from the original interview when the London Sun caught up with him a few weeks later.

His looks, and genuine musical abilities aside, Cassidy's greatest asset was his manager, former table tennis champion Ruth Aarons. He inherited her from his father, whose theatrical agent she had been. And while she knew precious little about Rock and Roll, she did understand the laws of Supply And Demand. Thus, when Screen Gems wanted David to make a third series of The Partridge Family, Ruth made certain it would make David a very rich man whether or not he ever worked again.

Whereas the Osmonds' career revolved as much around the decisions of Mike Curb at MGM as they did those of their official manager, Ed Leffler, Aarons cared for and protected David's interests with a jealous zeal. She knew that when David "retired" from the role of Keith Partridge at the end of the show's second series, public outrage alone would be enough to make the studio beg him to return. However, even she was surprised at just how great that public outrage was. "I got letters from fans asking if I'd stopped loving them," an incredulous Cassidy said. "They thought I was giving up the Partridge show because I'd stopped loving my fans."

Fairly early into his career as Keith Partridge, David took to working outside of the family group, turning the show's success into his own by persuading Bell Records (who distributed the group product) that he was talented enough — or adored enough, it didn't really matter which — to be launched as a performer in his own right. Together with Shirley Jones, he was the only member of the TV family who did actually sing on the group's records. Susan Dey, it was said, had a curious atonal voice, while the kids simply stood about looking bored every time the adults got down to the heavy stuff.

Indeed, even as a beginner, David evinced enough potential as a vocalist for Wes Farrell, the show's musical director (and co-author of Come On Down To My Boat, Baby), to abandon his original plan of bringing in some well-tried session singer to dub Keith's lines, and give the kid a break of his own.

Cassidy's first solo single, *Cherish*, was excellent even by the standards which the Partridges had set, a description

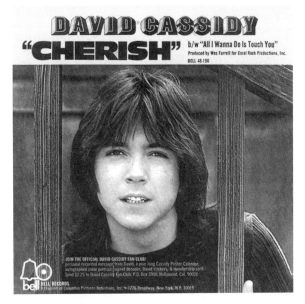

which also fits his first album, also titled CHERISH, released in 1972. Indeed, Cassidy's choice of material made the set a far more enduring selection than any of the Family's best known long playing offerings, if only because David, for the most part, was free of the constraints under which the Family labored. He even admits that musically, the most satisfying of all the Partridge albums were the last couple — BULLETIN BOARD and CROSSWORD PUZZLE, by which time he was the only person on the team who even seemed aware they existed.

"Wes had lost interest, Shirley had lost interest, so I just went in and went through the songbook, picked out the songs I wanted to cover, and did them. There was no pressure, no hassles, and (laughingly) no sales."

And while it was to be another three years before he was ever to be truly on his own, quitting the Bell label for RCA and releasing the prophetically titled THE HIGHER THEY CLIMB, THE HARDER THEY FALL album, even at his slushiest, Cassidy seldom let events stray far from his grasp. Recording through the late 1970's, moving into theater for the 80's, then dividing his time between the two through the 90's, Cassidy proved himself capable of meeting any challenge head on, and kicking it in the teeth.

The only exception to this rule — indeed, the event which persuaded Cassidy that it was finally time to take his leave of the teeny market — was the 1974 White City, London, concert where a young girl was fatally crushed. Cassidy was devastated, all the more so because he had already warned his advisors that such a tragedy was inevitable, given the hysteria whipped up by his every public appearance. With however many thousands of people so obviously out of control, it was simply a matter of time before someone got hurt. Within weeks of the concert, he had quit The Partridge Family. Within eighteen months, if the teen mags were anything to go by, he was forgotten. He later confessed he had never felt so happy in his life.

Discography:
Singles
- *I Think I Love You / Somebody Wants To Love You* (Bell 910, 1970)
- *Doesn't Somebody Want To Be Wanted? / You Are Always On My Mind* (Bell 963, 1971)
- *I'll Meet You Halfway / Morning Rider On The Road* (Bell 996, 1971)
- *I Woke Up In Love This Morning / 24 Hours A Day* (Bell 130, 1971)
- *It's One Of Those Nights / One Night Stand* (Bell 160, 1972)
- *Am I Losing You? / If You Ever Go* (Bell 200, 1972)
- *Breaking Up Is Hard To Do / I'm Here* (Bell 235, 1972)
- *Looking Thru The Eyes Of Love / Storybook Love* (Bell 301, 1973)
- *Friend And A Lover / Something's Wrong* (Bell 336, 1973)
- *Lookin' For A Good Time /* (Bell 414, 1973)

DAVID CASSIDY
Singles
- *Cherish / All I Wanna Do Is Touch You* (Bell 150, 1971)
- *Could It Be Forever? / Blind Hope* (Bell 187, 1972)
- *How Can I Be Sure? / Ricky's Tune* (Bell 220, 1972)
- *Rock Me Baby / Two Time Lover* (Bell 260, 1972)
- *Daydream / Can't Go Home Again* (Bell 386, 1973)
- *Please Please Me / Breaking Up Is Hard . . .* (Bell 605, 1974)
- *Get It Up For Love / Love In Bloom* (RCA 10321, 1975)
- *Darlin' / This Could Be The Night* (RCA 10405, 1975)
- *January / Junked Heart Blues* (RCA PB 9139, 1976)
- *Gettin' It In The Streets / I'll Have To Go Away* (RCA 10788, 1976)
- *Rosa's Cantina / Sayin' Goodbye Ain't Easy* (RCA 10921, 1977)

Albums
- CHERISH (Bell 6070, 1972)
- ROCK ME BABY (Bell 1109, 1973)
- DREAMS ARE NOTHING MORE THAN WISHES (Bell 1132, 1973)
- LIVE (Bell 1312, 1974)
- GREATEST HITS (Bell 1321, 1975)
- THE HIGHER THEY CLIMB (RCA 1066, 1975)
- HOME IS WHERE THE HEART IS (RCA 1307, 1975)
- GETTIN' IT IN THE STREETS (RCA 1852, 1976)

SHAUN CASSIDY
Singles
- *Da Doo Ron Ron / Holiday* (Warner / Curb 8365, 1977)
- *That's Rock'n'Roll / I Wanna Be With You* (Warner / Curb 8423, 1977)
- *Hey, Deanie / Strange Sensation* (Warner / Curb 8488, 1977)
- *Do You Believe In Magic? / Teen Dream* (Warner / Curb 8533, 1978)
- *Our Night / Right Before Your Eyes* (Warner / Curb 8634, 1978)
- *Midnight Sun / She's Right* (Warner / Curb 8698, 1978)
- *You're Usin' Me / You Still Surprise Me* (Warner / Curb 8859, 1979)

○ *Rebel Rebel* / (Warner / Curb 49568, 1980)
○ *Cool Fire* / *So Sad About Us* (Warner / Curb 49640, 1980)
Albums
○ SHAUN CASSIDY (Warner / Curb 3067, 1977)
○ BORN LATE (Warner / Curb 3126, 1977)
○ UNDER WRAPS (Warner / Curb 3222, 1978)
○ THAT'S ROCK'N'ROLL (Live) (Warner / Curb 3265, 1979)
○ ROOM SERVICE (Warner / Curb 3351, 1979)
○ WASP (Warner / Curb 3451, 1980)

SHIRLEY JONES
Singles
○ *I've Still Got My Heart, Joe* / (Bell 119, 1971)
○ *Ain't Love Easy* / (Bell 253, 1972)
○ *Walk In Silence* / (Bell 350, 1973)

RICKY SEGAL
Singles
○ *Sooner Or Later* / (Bell 429, 1974)

~ 20 ~
The Osmonds

1971: *One Bad Apple*

By 1970, The Osmond Brothers, a Mormon family hailing from Ogden, Utah, had been appearing as a four piece — the eldest of six performing brothers — on television for eight years. Discovered playing an impromptu set on a disused lot in Disneyland in 1962, they graduated to The Walt Disney Television Show, from there to The Andy Williams Show, and ultimately, The Jerry Lewis Show.

Not until 1970, however, did they sign a serious record contract. Hitherto, they said, they had been too busy with their television career to worry about records, and the four singles released to no applause in 1967-69, *I Can't Stop* (a worldwide hit upon reissue in 1974), *Mary Elizabeth*, *Lovin' On My Mind* and *Takin' A Chance On Love*, were to play no musical part in what the family was planning. For now, something seemed to be suggesting that the world was finally ready for their own peculiar brand of all-round family entertainment.

That "something" was the success of the Jacksons, and in particular, the omnipresence of little Michael. Augmenting their own line-up with 13 year old brother Donny, augmenting their sound with an adolescent falsetto lifted straight out of the Jacksons, the Osmonds rocketed to the top of the US chart with *One Bad Apple* in January, 1971. *Crazy Horses* annexed the rest of the world in late 1972 and, by 1973, the Osmonds were the biggest thing since sliced Beatles.

For starters, they were utterly faultless, vaguely super-human. They lived their lives free of drugs, free of alcohol, free of any artificial additives. As Mormons, their every action was dictated by their Church. They remained virgins until they were married, and when British journalist Charles Shaar Murray realized that the best musician in the band was also the only married one, his immediate reaction was to suggest the family's manager get them all hitched as soon as possible.

Everything about them was spotless. If ever a superstar was untouchable, it was the Osmonds. Over the next three years the Mormon Church was to win more converts than it ever could have done in the normal course of events. There was nothing insincere about them, nothing unpredictable or dangerous. The Beatles would have been okay to date, but you would never have wanted to actually settle down with one. Donny and Merrill and Alan, on the other hand, were sensitive and loving, safe and predictable. There was nothing crazy about them, not like those Monkees who'd promise to be true to you in one song, trade you in for a dog in the next. And if anybody doubted that sincerity, why, all they had to do was listen to the music.

It was the ultimate love affair. All that really mattered was that the idol existed, and existed on a plane where it didn't matter that you couldn't touch him, because neither could anybody else. Every girl dreamed of kissing Donny, of holding him and hugging him, but beyond that the mechanics of sex didn't really get a look in. Every detail of his family life was known, studied with an academic fervor which must have crippled any self respecting school teacher with envy. But more importantly, and this was where the teen mags came into their own, every aspect of the star's personal life, his past, his preferences, his destiny, was also open to scrutiny.

A lot of it was pure speculation, of course, the impoverished hack cobbling together half-remembered press releases and out-of-context one liners, but it was all presented with such style, such panache, that it was impossible to believe the magazine didn't have a direct line to The Adored One's heart.

"How to fall in love with Donny ... And make Donny fall in love with you" was a theme neither publisher nor public ever tired of. And if you didn't like Donny, well next week they'd tell you how to fall in love with David, with Michael, with anyone you could possibly want to fall in love with. Even Little Jimmy, the youngest Osmond of them all, was not spared.

Indeed, it was the teenybop press — in America 16 and Tiger Beat, in Britain Popswop and Music Star — which did the most to propagate the artists in the first place, keeping their names alive when the idols were out of sight, and saturating the news stands with them when they weren't. Glossy color photos and the stars' true confessions were only part of it. A subscription to Tiger Beat was like having a superstar pen pal. And if you ever got bored with writing to one, there were enough Osmonds on tap that you could have a new one every week.

The best of them all was probably Little Jimmy. A more precocious child could scarcely be imagined. Four years younger than Donny, he had already had a hit single (*Little Arrows*) — at the age of 5 — in Japan. Now, aged 9, he was set to unleash his follow-up, *Long Haired Lover From Liverpool*, and with Osmondmania now rivaling even the Beatles, the title was a timely jab in the Fab Four's eye. That aside, the strategy behind the release was breathtaking in its simplicity — and its effectiveness.

At 13 years of age, Donny was prime teen meat. The Mormon Church probably wouldn't have put it that way, while Ma and Pa Osmond were singularly unmanipulative in their dealings on the part of their sons. But one could never accuse their record company, MGM, of similar altruism, and the Osmonds' British invasion remains a casebook example of how to break a market without even breaking sweat.

Osmondmania hit the UK for the first time in the summer of 1972. *Down By The Lazy River*, a non-event of a single which had nevertheless given the brothers their third successive US Top Tenner a couple of months previous, had made a fleeting appearance in the British listings back in March, but the group were still something of an open secret as far as the country at large was concerned.

The cross-pollination of British and American charts was an exception, rather than a rule at that time, and were it not for The Osmonds' appearance at the annual Royal Command Performance, the single's success would have been regarded as nothing more than one of those peculiar little quirks which crop up from time to time for no particular reason.

But with MGM's press office now working flat out to ensure good notices for the brothers' debut, it wasn't long before the teen magazines picked up on the fact that, taken altogether, the boys really weren't that bad looking. And that was all it took.

The American success, in March, 1972, of Donny's *Puppy Love*, clinched it. It was his fourth US Top 10 hit and immediately the British press was canvassing MGM for a domestic release. The message of the song was perfect; "We're young, we're in love, and our folks say we'll grow out of it. Boy are they wrong."

The Osmonds

It was a theme Donny had already aired a few times in the past. Indeed it was one trotted out by every teenaged balladeer who ever lived. But with the UK charts already showing signs of succumbing to a serious weirdness which would do nothing for the sales of the pop-oriented glossies, even the most hackneyed theme was welcome if it would help stop the rot. And besides, the boy was cute.

In June 1972, MGM bowed to "public pressure" and released *Puppy Love* in Britain. It went straight to No.1, and stayed there for five weeks. By the time the Osmonds announced that they were returning to London in the fall, the publicity machine had been running on auto-pilot for close on six months. The group's arrival at London Heathrow was witnessed by nigh on 10,000 screaming fans, and while rumor had it that many of them had been paid off by promo men anxious to curry favor with America's first family of pop, there is no doubt that the hysteria — which had even the hardest newsmen phoning through reports of Beatlemania (part two) — was very genuine.

A chant taken up at one end of the airport would communicate itself to the other within seconds. Periodically, everyone would scream for no reason whatsoever. Touts wandering through the crowd selling cheapo pins and lurex scarves could hardly believe their luck — normally, record companies frown upon that sort of thing. This time around, they didn't even seem to care.

Radio Luxembourg, who had done so much to publicize the band's arrangements over the previous week, later claimed that both Elton John and the Jackson Five had flown into Heathrow immediately ahead of the Osmonds and had been all but ignored by the waiting masses. "The screams were quite astonishing, frightening," wrote journalist Mike Ledgerwood. "The return of the new teeny idol is here. A new generation of fans has now arrived . . . The SCREAMAGERS."

And it wasn't only Heathrow which was under siege. The Finsbury Park Rainbow, where the Osmonds were to appear, became a camp site for three nights worth of teenaged girls, all hoping to be among the lucky first ticket buyers who would receive a free Osmonds LP for their troubles. And from there they rushed to the Churchill Hotel, where, Radio Luxembourg DJ Tony Prince inadvertently let slip, the band would be staying. When someone asked him why he said it, Prince replied, "Nobody told me not to." It was a genuine mistake — or at least as genuine a mistake as could be made in a campaign which had been planned down to the last bathroom stop.

November 3, 1972, saw war declared on three very separate fronts. For the rockers there was the Osmonds' *Crazy Horses*; for the romantics there was Donny's *Why*, and for everybody else, Grandmothers to Grandchildren, there was little James Arthur Osmond.

In America, where the fervor was already beginning to die down, this unholy trinity caused more trouble than it was worth with *Why* and *Crazy Horses* peaking at 13 and 14 respectively, and *Long Haired Lover* making a brief appearance way down the ladder at number 38. Britain, however, simply lapped it up, then came back begging for more. Jimmy reached No. 1, the boys got to No. 2, Donny to No. 3. Not since the heyday of the Beatles had any one group been so dominant, but at least they had had the decency not to drag out the rest of the family to share in the fun. Suddenly the Osmonds stopped being the joke most "serious" pop fans had labeled them as. Now they were a threat.

With only a handful of variations, the show which the Osmonds brought to Britain for their fourteen day visit in 1972 was to remain constant for the next three years. The greatest hits sequence, the Karate sequence, the Rock and Roll medley, it never really changed.

And it was, perhaps, this refusal to move with the times which led ultimately to the Osmonds' downfall. Even at 17, Donny was still too young to love. Little Jimmy at 14 was as pugnacious as Little Jimmy at 9, the only real difference being, he was no longer so little. And the band as a whole had done themselves no favors when they unleashed THE PLAN, a monolithic concept album outlining their philosophical beliefs. The little girls didn't care a fig for what the Osmonds thought about the state of the planet. They wanted to know what the Osmonds thought about them.

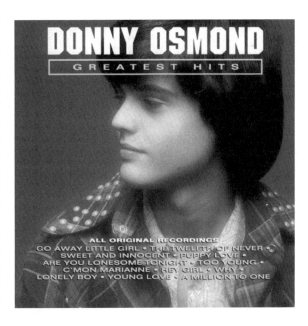

With any audience beyond that which they had already won steadfastly refusing to even acknowledge the Osmonds' existence, suddenly the brothers had painted themselves into a musical corner from which nothing more than a complete change of direction could liberate them. And while the hysteria died down almost overnight, their greatest achievement of the past 25 years has been the ease with which they accomplished this, first by switching their attentions to the country circuit, then by putting up no more than a token resistance to the widespread coverage which sister Olive Marie's ill-starred marriage was to receive. It was as if by proving themselves to be less than superhuman after all, they would at last be able to return to earth. Donny and Marie's television comeback aside, most people today couldn't even name the individual Osmond brothers.

Discography:
Singles
- *Be My Little Baby Bumble Bee / I Wouldn't Trade The Silver In My Mother's Hair* (MGM 13162, 1963)
- *The Travels Of Jamie Mcpheeters / Aura Lee* (MGM 13174, 1963)
- *Mr. Sandman / My Mom* (MGM 13281, 1964)
- *I Can't Stop / Flower Music* (UNI 55015, 1967)
- *Mary Elizabeth / Speak Like A Child* (Barnaby 2002, 1968)

- *I've Got Loving On My Mind / Mollie A* (Barnaby 2004, 1968)
- *Takin' A Chance On Love / Groove With What You Got* (Barnaby 2005, 1969)
- *Movin' Along / Movin' Along* (MGM 14159, 1970)
- *One Bad Apple / He Ain't Heavy . . .* (MGM 14193, 1970)
- *Double Lovin' / Chilly Winds* (MGM 14259, 1971)
- *YoYo / Keep On My Side* (MGM 14295, 1971)
- *Down By The Lazy River / He's The Light Of The World* (MGM 14324, 1972)
- *Hold Her Tight / Love Is* (MGM 14405, 1972)
- *We Can Make It Together / E Fini* (MGM 14383, 1972)
- *Crazy Horses / That's My Girl* (MGM 14450, 1972)
- *Going Home / Are You Up There* (MGM 14562, 1973)
- *Let Me In / One Way Ticket* (MGM 14617, 1973)
- *I Can't Stop / Flower Music* (UNI 55276, 1974)
- *Love Me For A Reason / Fever* (MGM 14746, 1974)
- *The Proud One / The Last Day Is Coming* (MGM 14791, 1975)
- *I'm Still Gonna Need You / Thank You* (MGM 14831, 1975)
- *I Can't Live A Dream / Check It Out* (Polydor 14348, 1976)

Albums
- OSMONDS (MGM 4724, 1970)
- HOMEMADE (MGM 4770, 1971)
- PHASE III (MGM 4796, 1971)
- LIVE (MGM 4826, 1972)
- CRAZY HORSES (MGM 4851, 1972)
- THE PLAN (MGM 4902, 1973)
- LOVE ME FOR A REASON (MGM 4939, 1974)
- THE PROUD ONE (MGM 4993, 1975)
- AROUND THE WORLD — IN CONCERT (MGM 5012, 1976)
- BRAINSTORM (MGM 6077, 10 / 7)
- CHRISTMAS ALBUM (Polydor 8001, 1977)
- GREATEST HITS (Polydor 9005, 1978)

DONNY OSMOND
Singles
- *Sweet And Innocent / Flirtin'* (MGM 14227, 1971)
- *Go Away Little Girl / Time To Ride* (MGM 14285, 1971)
- *Hey Girl / I Knew You When* (MGM 14322, 1971)
- *Puppy Love / Let My People Go* (MGM 14367, 1972)
- *Too Young / Love Me* (MGM 14407, 1972)
- *Why / Lonely Boy* (MGM 14424, 1972)
- *Twelfth Of Never / Life Is Just What You Make It* (MGM 14503, 1973)
- *Young Love / Million To One* (MGM 14583, 1973)
- *Are You Lonesome Tonight? / When I Fall In Love* (MGM 14677, 1973)
- *I Have A Dream / I'm Dyin'* (MGM 14781, 1974)
- *C'mon Marianne / I Got Your Loving* (Polydor 14320, 1976)
- *Danglin' On A String / I'm Sorry* (Polydor 14417, 1977)

Albums
- THE DONNY OSMOND ALBUM (MGM 4782, 1971)
- TO YOU WITH LOVE (MGM 4797, 1971)
- PORTRAIT OF DONNY (MGM 4820, 1972)
- TOO YOUNG (MGM 4854, 1972)
- MY BEST TO YOU (MGM 4872, 1972)
- ALONE TOGETHER (MGM 4886, 1973)
- A TIME FOR US (MGM 4930, 1973)
- DONNY (MGM 4978, 1975)
- DISCOTRAIN (Polydor 6067, 1976)
- DONALD CLARKE OSMOND (Polydor 6109, 1977)

DONNY & MARIE OSMOND
Singles
- *I'm Leaving It All Up To You / The Umbrella Song* (MGM 14735, 1974)
- *Morning Side Of The Mountain / One Of These Days* (MGM 14765, 1974)
- *Make The World Go Away / Livin' On My Suspicion* (MGM 14807, 1975)
- *Deep Purple / Take Me Back Again* (MGM 14840, 1976)
- *Ain't Nothing Like The Real Thing / Sing* (Polydor 14363, 1976)
- *Soul And Inspiration / Now We're Together* (Polydor 14339, 1978)
- *Baby I'm Sold On You / Sure Would Be Nice* (Polydor 14456, 1978)
- *On The Shelf / Certified Honey* (Polydor 14510, 11 / 7)
Albums
- I'M LEAVING IT ALL UP TO YOU (MGM 4968, 1974)
- MAKE THE WORLD GO AWAY (MGM 4996, 1975)
- SING SONGS FROM THEIR TV SHOW (Polydor 6068, 1976)
- NEW SEASON (Polydor 6083, 1976)
- WINNING COMBINATION (Polydor 6127, 1978)
- GOING COCONUTS (Polydor 6169, 1978)

JIMMY OSMOND
Singles
- *If Santa Was My Daddy / Silent Night* (MGM 14328, 1972)
- *Long Haired Lover From Liverpool / Mother Of Mine* (MGM 14376, 1972)
- *Tweedle Dee / Mama'd Know* (MGM 14668, 1973)
- *Give Me A Good Old Mammy Song /* (MGM 14687, 1974)
- *Yes Virginia, There Is A Santa Claus /* (MGM 14770, 1974)
- *Little Arrows / Don't You Remember* (MGM 14771, 1974)
Albums
- KILLER JOE (MGM 4855, 1973)
- LITTLE ARROWS (MGM 4916, 1974)

MARIE OSMOND
Singles
- *Paper Roses / Least Of All You* (MGM 14609, 1973)
- *In My Little Corner Of The World / The Other Way Round* (MGM 14694, 1974)
- *Who's Sorry Now / This I Promise You* (MGM 14786, 1975)

- *Weeping Willow* / (Polydor 14333, 1977)
- *This Is The Way That I Feel* / *Play The Music Loud* (Polydor 14385, 1977)
- *Please Tell Him I Said Hello* / (Polydor 14405, 1977)

Albums
- PAPER ROSES (MGM 4910, 1973)
- IN MY LITTLE CORNER OF THE WORLD (MGM 4944, 1974)
- WHO'S SORRY NOW (MGM 4979, 1975)
- THIS IS THE WAY THAT I FEEL (Polydor 6099, 1977)

~ 21 ~
The Carpenters

1971: *Superstar*

Take two California siblings, cleaner than clean, smoother than smooth, toothpaste admen with strings and pianos . . . looking back over the years of chocolate box marketing, even Richard Carpenter cannot suppress a shudder. "We were getting skewered by the critics, and if you look at [our] LP covers, you can't blame them. Cheek to cheek, it's just too sweet . . ." and then you cut to the action, another prime time special, an early 70's video clip, and you wonder what would he have preferred? Leather, raunch and Spinal Tap? The Carpenters were sweet, and if there was something decaying beneath the surface, then it only proves how sweet they were, that they continued smiling while they rotted away.

Documenting the Carpenters rise from garageland prodigies in the early 1960's, to mega-platinum superstars just a decade later, and onto a finale so chilling it's still hard to comprehend, is a sobering pastime. Songwriter Richard may look like a grinning game show host, or a put upon 60's sitcom husband, but recent years and TV documentaries alike have seen him delve into what are clearly some difficult memories and somehow come up smiling every time.

Sister Karen's death, from the then barely understood anorexia, did more than derail a monstrously successful career, after all. It also shattered his own life, and he would be the first to admit that since then, he's done little more than live in the shadow of all that the duo created through the first half of the 70's. And if he sometimes seems a little cynical, about the wealth of retro adoration which the Carpenters have accumulated in the last five or six years, and the woodwork straining emergence of countless closet admirers, that, too, is only to be expected. Like he says, at the time, the critics skewered them. Cheek to cheek . . .

The Carpenters were never going to be hip, no matter how desperately they tried to be. Fuzz drenched axe parts, Leon Russell groupie songs, they threw everything apart from a garage rock tantrum. But throughout their early-mid 1970's heyday they were, and they remained, the grinny toothed antithesis to even the lightest weight AORocker, and when the early 90's finally saw them achieve the Hip Young Blade breakthrough that they'd always craved, it was from quarters as lo fi as the Carpenters themselves were hi ... Sonic Youth's Carpenters tribute album.

For once, however, the twists of taste were on the right track. The Carpenters made fabulous records, exquisitely crafted masterpieces which remain as much a part of the 70's experience as any of the hot young hipsters who the critics didn't smirk at. Even at their most calculatedly smug (and *Sing*, with its crafted kiddy chorus is certainly that), there's an irresistible effervescence to the duo's music which even gut-

wrenching hatred cannot completely subvert. And of course, the girl sure could sing.

Richard and Karen Carpenter's career can be boiled down into three largely self contained periods. First came the years spent refining the sound and honing the image. Then there was the era of increasing super stardom, and increasing ambition to match. And finally, there was the decline, starting slowly, but snowballing fearlessly, getting faster and faster, interestingly enough, as the chart positions got lower and lower.

Raised in New Haven Connecticut, the Carpenters formed in the late 1960's in Downy, California following their family's cross-country move. There, Richard began studying piano, Karen took up drums, and for a time, the pair worked with bassist Wes Jacobs in a trio which cut a couple of flop singles for the local Magic Lamp label. They also won a Battle of the Bands contest at the Hollywood Bowl in 1967, first prize a deal with RCA. As the Richard Carpenter Trio, they cut four songs before the band fell apart and the Carpenters (with guitarist John Betties) formed a new group, Spectrum. Spectrum, too, collapsed, and

The Carpenters

the Carpenters began performing as a duo, in which form they cut a demo tape with Los Angeles session musician Joe Osborn. A copy found its way to A&M Records chief Herb Alpert, and in early 1969, he signed the Carpenters to his label.

1969's debut, *Ticket To Ride*, was largely a slab of disposable schmaltz, notable only for what would become its title track (the album was originally released as OFFERING, then retitled after the duo's first hit), and a cover of Fifth Dimension's *Magic Garden*; while the new year's CLOSE TO YOU — its title track the group's first US number one — retained enough of its predecessor's chocolate box flimsiness that even its moments of most sublime beauty (*Close To You, We've Only Just Begun*, and a spellbinding *Reason To Believe*) still barely hint at the talents which would soon be unleashed.

That moment came with 1971's eponymous third album, recorded in the euphoric heat which followed the duo winning a Grammy as Best New Act of 1970. Excise the Vegas grotesqueries of the Bacharach / David medley, a hangover from its predecessors' insecurities, and CARPENTERS is close to being a masterpiece. Riding in on two superlative hits (*For All We Know* and *Rainy Days And Mondays*) and tickling the funny bone with Richard's showcase *Druscilla Penny*, it finally attained perfection with *Superstar*, the most breathtaking Carpenters' performance of all. From there on in, Karen's status as THE premier vocal stylist of her generation was unimpeachable.

And it's true — even the briefest flirtation with the siblings' subsequent catalog is going to be defined by Karen's emotional impact. *Good-bye To Love, Yesterday Once More, Hurting Each Other*, even a fairly mundane rendition of Neil Sedaka's *Solitaire*, all topped one chart or another on the strength of the palpable sorrow she conveyed in a sigh. *Jambalaya* became a quite unlikely UK smash on the buoyancy of her joy, and a few album only items call out with siren like allure, to lure the listener away from a simple hits collection.

HORIZON's touching stroll through the Eagles' *Desperado* suffered by comparison with Linda Ronstadt's near simultaneous rendering, but still wiped the floor with the Eagles' cold fish original. NOW AND THEN's *This Masquerade* sounded so choked that it was almost too painful to listen to all the way through. And from the same album, *End Of The World* physically teetered on the edge of heartbroken apocalypse. Perhaps it's just as well the song was slice'n'diced into a side-long oldies radio pastiche (complete with annoying DJ impressions.) Leonard Cohen had enough competition already at that time.

Released in January, 1973, NOW AND THEN was the sound of the Carpenters hitting their creative peak. THE SINGLES, later that same year, saw them do the same in commercial terms. Their first American chart topper, the album stayed on the British chart for 125 weeks, and ruled that roost for 17. They were, like the song says, "On Top Of The World" and it would take almost a decade until tragedy told the world precisely how they came to fall from there so heavily.

The decline manifested itself slowly. Neither HORIZONS (1975) nor A KIND OF HUSH (1976) were too bad, with Karen's obvious love for *Please Mr. Postman* jollying up an otherwise well overdone arrangement. Similarly, 1977's otherwise flaccid PASSAGE was dominated by *Don't Cry For Me Argentina* proudly crowning an "Evita" medley, and a bafflingly lovely cover of Klaatu's *Calling Occupants Of Interplanetary Craft*. But even at what now passed for their best, the instinctive sincerity which had once been so much a part of the duo's magic was audibly draining away.

By the end of the decade, the Carpenters had effectively broken up, with Karen breaking away to record a solo album — then returning to the fold when A&M announced they wouldn't be releasing it. But 1981's MADE IN AMERICA ended a four year recorded silence by making even devoted fans wish it had been a five year one. And though Karen's death in February, 1983, allowed VOICE OF THE HEART at least a little sentimental leeway at the time, distance proves the poignancy was all in the listener's mind. The album itself is dull as ditch water, and its absolute under-representation on the otherwise authoritative YESTERDAY ONCE MORE compilation proves that Richard thinks so, as well.

The Carpenters, to borrow a cliché which they were never cut out for, lived fast and died young, literally and figuratively. But the music they made has proved so marvelously immortal that one can almost forgive them for proving so tragically human themselves.

Discography:
Singles
- *I'll Be Yours / Looking For Love* (Magic Lamp 704, 1967)
- *Ticket To Ride / Your Wonderful Parade* (A&M 1142, 1969)
- *Close To You / I Kept On Loving You* (A&M 1183, 1970)
- *We've Only Just Begun / All Of My Life* (A&M 1217, 1970)
- *Merry Christmas Darling / Mr. Guder* (A&M 1236, 1970)
- *For All We Know / Don't Be Afraid* (A&M 1243, 1971)
- *Rainy Days And Mondays / Saturday* (A&M 1260, 1971)
- *Superstar / Bless The Beasts And Children* (A&M 1289, 1971)
- *Hurting Each Other / Maybe It's You* (A&M 1322, 1972)
- *It's Going To Take Some Time / Flat Baroque* (A&M 1351, 1972)
- *Goodbye To Love / Crystal Lullaby* (A&M 1367, 1972)
- *Top Of The World / Druscilla Penny* (A&M 1391, 1972)
- *Sing / Druscilla Penny* (A&M 1413, 1973)
- *Yesterday Once More / Road Ode* (A&M 1446, 1973)
- *Top Of The World / Heather* (A&M 1468, 1973)
- *I Won't Last A Day Without You / One Love* (A&M 1521, 1974)
- *Please Mr. Postman / This Masquerade* (A&M 1646, 1974)
- *Santa Claus Is Coming To Town / Merry Christmas* (A&M 1648, 1974)
- *Only Yesterday / Happy* (A&M 1677, 1975)
- *Solitaire / Love Me For What I Am* (A&M 1721, 1975)
- *There's A Kind Of Hush / Goodbye And I Love You* (A&M 1800, 1976)

- *I Need To Be In Love / Sandy* (A&M 1828, 1976)
- *Goofus / Boat To Sail* (A&M 1859, 1976)
- *All You Get From Love / I Have You* (A&M 1940, 1977)
- *Calling Occupants Of Interplanetary Craft / Can't Smile Without You* (A&M 1978, 1977)
- *Christmas Song / Merry Christmas Darling* (A&M 1991, 1977)
- *Sweet Sweet Smile / I Have You* (A&M 2008, 1978)
- *I Believe You / Bwana She No Home* (A&M 2097, 1978)
- *Touch Me When We're Dancing / Because We Are In Love* (A&M 2344, 1981)
- *Back In My Life Again / Somebody's Been Lyin'* (A&M 2370, 1981)
- *Those Good Ol' Dreams / When It's Gone* (A&M 2386, 1981)
- *Beechwood 4-5789 / Two Sides* (A&M 2405, 1982)
- *Make Believe It's Your First Time / Look To Your Dreams* (A&M 2585, 1983)

Albums
- TICKET TO RIDE (A&M 4205, 1969)
- CLOSE TO YOU (A&M 4271, 1970)
- CARPENTERS (A&M 3502, 1971)
- A SONG FOR YOU (A&M 3511, 1972)
- NOW AND THEN (A&M 3519, 1973)
- THE SINGLES 1969-73 (A&M 3601, 1973)
- HORIZON (A&M 4530, 1975)
- A KIND OF HUSH (A&M 4581, 1976)
- PASSAGE (A&M 4703, 1977)
- CHRISTMAS PORTRAIT (A&M 4726, 1978)
- MADE IN AMERICA (A&M 3723, 1981)
- VOICE OF THE HEART (A&M 4954, 1983)

~ 22 ~
Bubblerock

1972: *Satisfaction*

Imagine, if you will, Bill Haley's *Rock Around The Clock*, performed as a waltz. Contemplate, if you can, *Mr. Tambourine Man*, rearranged for 15 tambourines. And finally, if your stomach is still up to it, consider the Supremes' *Reflections*, if it thought it was *Whole Lotta Love*."

Congratulations. You have just visualized BUBBLEROCK IS HERE TO STAY, the first, and (some might say mercifully) only album ever released by Bubblerock, a British band whose name so aggressively summed up their music that they didn't actually need to make records. The mere threat would have ensured world domination.

Issued in 1972 through London Records, BUBBLEROCK IS HERE TO STAY was, in fact, the first full length release from Britain's UK records, a company which would go on to launch both 10cc and Jona Lewie (as Terry Dactyl and the Dinosaurs) on their hit making careers, but was better known at the time for its founder, Jonathan King — probably the most ubiquitous hit maker in the history of British pop.

Between 1965, when the 17 year old King scored his first smash single, and 1979, when he wrapped up 15 years of recording making with the aptly titled HIT MILLIONAIRE album, King was responsible for well over a score of UK chart busters, and a few American ones as well, beginning with his own *Everyone's Gone To The Moon*, recorded while the erstwhile Kenneth King was still a student at Trinity College, Cambridge.

It is an impressive career, rivaled by only a handful of other acts, yet check King's entry in the British Guinness Book Of Hit Singles, and the evidence really isn't there. A couple of Top Five singles ten years apart, five more lowly Top 30 entries, and a couple of bottom tenners . . . so what? It's the "see also . . ." footnote which you have to pay attention to, and even that only begins to tell the story. Hedgehoppers Anonymous, the Weathermen, the Piglets, Sakharin, 53rd And 3rd, Father Abraphart and the Smurps, Sound 9418, 100 Tons And A Feather, Shag, Bubblerock, Nemo . . . musically he was a genius, but his detractors — and there are a great many of them — preferred to regard him as a cretin.

Good News Week, written and produced for Hedgehoppers Anonymous in 1965, was a multipurpose protest song concocted by King as the deformed step brother of Barry McGuire's *Eve Of Destruction*. But while McGuire sang as if he really meant it (or at least, as if he wished he meant it), Hedgehoppers, whom King had transformed from an Air Force band called the Trendsetters, evinced all the social concern of a three year old — which was precisely who Jonathan was aiming the record at. And the next one, and the next one . . .

Under a bewildering variety of guises, King spent the next decade and a half first spotting, then exploiting every crack in Great Britain's musical armor. And the crasser it was, the better. His version of *Sugar Sugar*, recorded under the name Sakharin in 1971, quite mercilessly employed every trick in the Heavy Metal song book, right down to the sub-Hendrix guitar which warbled the hookline. *Johnny Reggae*, ostensibly by the all-girl Piglets, immortalized every girl who ever hung around on street corners eyeing up the skinheads. Even 10cc's *Donna*, released as it was on King's UK label, was initially regarded as just another of Jonathan's little hoaxes.

As assistant to Sir Kenneth Clarke, director of Decca Records, King discovered, named and produced Genesis, and their early reputation suffered accordingly. But his heart belonged to throwaway pop, and throughout his time at Decca, King was afforded unlimited studio time, from whence he was to emerge with four quite astonishing singles.

The best was without doubt his violent cover of B.J. Thomas' *Hooked On A Feeling*, a song whose predominant musical message was a repeated refrain of "Oogachucka, ooga-ooga-ooga chucka . . ." Three years later, Blue Swede did much the same thing, but King's had a demented edge ("ooga "CHUCKA") which his successors never even contemplated. The worst, on the other hand, was the lackadaisical *Flirt*, the weirdest was *Lazybones*, and the hippest was *Let It All Hang Out*.

All four were released under King's own name and all four were hits. Indeed, on two occasions in 1971, he had no less than three singles on the British chart simultaneously. in the spring, *Lazybones* and *Sugar Sugar* were joined by St. Cecilia's delightful *Leap Up And Down, Wave Your Knickers In The Air*, which he produced. Later, in the fall, his production of the Bay City Rollers' *Keep On Dancing* was going down the chart as *Hooked On A Feeling* and *Johnny Reggae* were moving up it. And he admits, quite openly, that the only reason he does release so many records under so many names is so that he'll get more airplay, and hopefully, more hits.

Upon leaving Decca in 1970, King quickly set about establishing himself first as an independent producer, then as a record company mogul in his own right. In August 1972, he produced Mardi Gras' *Too Busy Thinking 'Bout My Baby*, at the same time as launching the UK label into the British chart with Terry Dactyl's *Seaside Shuffle*.

From there, King threw his all into UK, and over the next few years racked up an astonishing amount of success. Licensing Roy C's 60's soul classic *Shotgun Wedding* was a masterstroke which gave UK both a hit and a certain amount of grudging admiration from folk who still considered King to be tone deaf. He then reversed that process with the maniacal *Loop Di Love* — recorded under sexually suggestive, and very pre-Austin Powers, name of Shag — a No. 4 hit which was subtly reborn a decade later as Dexy's Midnight Runners' *Come On Eileen*. At one point UK was operating on a hit ratio of one in ten, at a time when most record companies considered themselves to be doing extraordinarily well if they managed one in twenty! Only Micky Most's RAK was doing better.

Bubblerock finally arrived in 1972, a musically audacious concept which the liner notes only partially explained: "it's the easiest thing in the world to look back on a great old sound and remember how much you loved it. [But] a rehearing can only bring nostalgia." In order for the song to live again, it needed to be reinvented. "Which is why the music industry has given birth to Bubblerock."

So, "the million sellers as never heard before." But did Leslie Gore's *It's My Party* really require the addition of the words "boo hoo" to the line "I'll cry if I want to"? Did *Have I The Right* really deserve to sound like Deep Purple? And was the Stones' *Satisfaction* necessarily a suitable candidate for the country folk treatment? Probably not, although that wasn't enough to stop it appearing as a single two years later, and marching straight into the British Top 30.

Did Bubblerock stir again? Nobody seems sure. There may have been an unsuccessful follow up single, a similarly reworked *19th Nervous Breakdown*, but any trace of its existence appears to have been obliterated. In any case, King himself ensured the whole thing was swiftly forgotten as he unleashed a fresh deluge of hits and pseudonyms in 1975.

When Dutch singing group Pussycat had a hit with *Mississippi*, King was out there counseling the British people to be patriotic and buy his own version instead. When the George Baker Selection threatened to have a hit with the implausibly bland *Una Paloma Blanca*, King preempted them with an even blander rendering. A tentative Glenn Miller revival, spearheaded by *Moonlight Serenade*'s return to the British chart, was celebrated by Sound 9418's *In The Mood*. And the American success of Tavares' *It Only Takes A Minute* was echoed in Britain by 100 Tons And A Feather's psychotic violin led reappraisal.

The Sex Pistols released *God Save The Queen* in June 1977. King retaliated with *God Save The Sex Pistols*, by "Elizabeth R.," simultaneously doing the Pistols' cause irreparable damage with the line "Anarchist, anarchist, anarchist the girl next door." And when Britain and its petroleum industry were suddenly smitten by those loathsome elf-things, the Smurfs, and their human friend Father Abraham, King struck back with Father Abraphart & The Smurps' condemnation of leaded gasoline — *Lick A Smurp For Christmas (All Fall Down)*.

And so it went on. Through the 1980's, King hosted a marvelous "letter from America" type TV program, Entertainment USA. Today, he remains the supreme arbiter of British taste (or otherwise), as the head of the committee which picks the UK's entrant for the annual Eurovision Song Contest. In 1997, he chose a song called *Love Shine A Light*. Performed by the Anglo American Katrina and the Waves, it won by the highest margin in Eurovision's 40+ year history.

King's impact on the British pop scene, then, is obvious. In borrowing from Kasenatz-Katz (and Jefferson Airplane) the basic principle that "No Man Is An Island — He's An Archipelago," King has shown time and time again that not only is it possible to fool all of the people all of the time, most of the people actually enjoy being fooled. With almost mathematical precision, he worked out the lowest common denominator in public taste and built an empire around it. And while Bubblegum purists no doubt ridicule him as much as everybody else, still there is no doubting one thing — thanks to Jonathan King, Bubblerock really was here to stay.

Discography:
Singles (Jonathan King)
- *Everyone's Gone To The Moon / Summer's Coming* (Parrot 9774, 1965)
- *Where The Sun Has Never Shone / Green . . . Grass* (Parrot 9804, 1966)
- *Just Like A Woman / Land Of The Golden Tree* (Parrot 3005, 1967)
- *Icicles / In A Hundred Years From Now* (Parrot 3008, 1967)
- *Round Round / Time And Motion* (Parrot 3011, 1967)
- *Message To The Political Candidates / Colloquial Sex* (Parrot 3021, 1968)
- *Lazy Bones / I Just Want To Say Thank You* (Parrot 3027, 1971)

- *Hooked On A Feeling* / *I Don't Want To Be Gay* (Parrot 3029, 1971)
- *Flirt* / *Hey Jim* (Parrot 3030, 1972)
- *Learned Tax Council* / *Tall Order For A Short Guy* (UK 49002, 1973)
- *Mary My Love* / *Tall Order For A Short Guy* (UK 49014, 1974)
- *The Kung Fu Anthem* / *A Little Bit Left Of Right* (UK 49018, 1974)
- *The Way You Look Tonight* / *Molly Malone* (UK 49034, 1975)
- *Una Paloma Blanca* / (Big Tree 16046, 1975)

~ 23 ~
Tony Orlando And Dawn

1973: *Tie A Yellow Ribbon Round The Ole Oak Tree*

According to front man Tony Orlando, the members of Dawn were complete strangers when they cut the group's first record. But it didn't show. *Candida* burst onto the American (and later, British) chart in 1970 with a freshness, a verve and yes, an intimacy, which defied any attempt to belittle it — even Orlando's other acknowledgment, that the group itself was simply another session opportunity when it first came along, and that nobody involved ever had any idea that it would end up so fabulously successful. A gorgeous sing-along, a compulsive grin, and a melody sharp enough to shave with, *Candida* was one of those records which was simply so catchy that there was no way it could fail. That Dawn would go on to dwarf its achievements on at least two other occasions, simply proves that some successes cannot be calculated. They just happen, despite themselves.

Michael Anthony Orlando Cassivitis got his start performing and recording demos with such local, New York City, doo-wop groups as the Five Gents, then hanging round the Brill Building in the hope of getting a tape to someone who worked there. Don Kirshner was the lucky first recipient. He linked Orlando with Carole King and Gerry Goffin to record one of their songs, *Halfway to Paradise* (Kirshner produced) and in 1960, Orlando found himself with his first Top 40 hit.

Barry Mann and Cynthia Weill's *Bless You* followed, hitting No. 15 in the US and a commendable No. 5 in the UK in late 1961. But when Kirshner sold his company to Screen Gems, Orlando's recording career ground to a halt, and by 1963, he was working in music publishing, first at Robbins, Feist and Miller, then at April-Blackwood, where he handled the catalogs of James Taylor and Laura Nyro. And there he might have remained had producers Medress and Appell not called him in to replace the lead vocalist in a Detroit-based trio they were leading through a song called *Candida*. Without ever meeting his bandmates, whose parts were recorded in California, Orlando lay down his vocals, convinced that the song would never be heard of again. Instead, it became the biggest hit of his career so far, and within two months, Orlando had quit his music publishing job and joined Dawn full time.

Like Orlando, the remainder of the Dawn team also had impressive careers as undeserving under-achievers behind them. Telma Louise Hopkins and Joyce Vincent Wilson were ex-Motown backing vocalists (their credits included Marvin Gaye's *I Heard It Through the Grapevine*, Freda Payne's *Band Of Gold* and Isaac Hayes' *Theme From Shaft*), and producers Dave Appell and Hank Medress (a former member of *Lion Sleeps Tonight* hit makers the Tokens) were precisely that, producers. But naming the band after Bell Records boss Wes Farrell's daughter, Dawn, and picking *Candida* for their first release was more than simple good fortune. It was a decision which would redraw the boundaries of pop through the 1970's.

Candida entered the chart in August. By September, it had sold over a million records. And while it could only reach No. 3, the next four years saw Dawn run up three No. 1's of such magnitude that today one of them, *Tie A Yellow Ribbon Round The Old Oak Tree*, remains an integral part of America's popular culture.

Five million-selling singles, six Top Ten hits, two platinum albums, a network variety show, a pair of American Music Awards and two Grammy nominations completed Dawn's role of honor. And if the critics hated Dawn's flimsy bubblegum sound, it may have come as a surprise to them to learn that Orlando kind of agreed with them. "I kept wondering who would listen to that crap," he told Newsweek once. But not only did they listen to it, they bought in, all around the world, and in ever increasing quantities. By the time Dawn split, they had sold over 30 million records.

With an album quickly coming together, CANDIDA, Dawn's attention turned to their next single, the mighty *Knock Three Times*. It made No. 1 in both the US and UK, the prelude to a series of hits which saw Dawn seldom leave the Top 40 — *I Play And Sing*, *Summer Sand* and the spirited *What Are You Doing Sunday*.

A second, self-titled, Dawn album flopped, but the group's third LP, 1973's TUNEWEAVING, proved to be the monster that the trio's singles success had long been threatening. It also gave birth to a monster of its own, *Tie A Yellow Ribbon Round The Ole Oak Tree*. The song itself was about a recently freed jailbird, returning home to find out whether his old love still wanted him — if she did, she was to tie the ribbon round the tree. If he didn't see it, he'd just stay on the bus ... all of which must have sent a worrisome message to the American POWs returning home from the Vietnam War, just as the song hit its peak. Still, *Tie A Yellow Ribbon* became the anthem of the moment (just as it would still be, nearly 20 years later following the Gulf War) and again Dawn had a trans-Atlantic chart topper.

Tony Orlando And Dawn

Voted Favorite Single, Pop-Rock at the first-ever American Music Awards in 1973, and nominated for two Grammy Awards Song Of The Year and Best Pop Group Performance, *Tie A Yellow Ribbon* sold more than six million copies worldwide.

Dawn's CBS television series, Tony Orlando and Dawn, was originally scheduled to run for just four weeks through the summer. It ended up surviving two full seasons, and gave Orlando, at least, the opportunity to live out one of his own personal dreams, to engineer a revival, or at least modernization, of old-time ragtime / big band music. With the *Yellow Ribbon* writing team of Levine and Brown behind him, Orlando led Dawn through a string of increasingly surreal, but completely flawless, swing-style smashes, *Say, Has Anybody Seen My Sweet Gypsy Rose*, *Who's In The Strawberry Patch With Sally*, *Steppin Out (Gonna Boogie Tonight)*, *Look In My Eyes Pretty Woman* and 1975's *He Don't Love You (Like I Love You)*, Dawn's third No. 1 single.

It was also their last major hit. Through 1976-77, Dawn's singles met with ever-decreasing returns. *Mornin' Beautiful* reached No. 14; *You're All I Need To Get By* (originally a hit for Marvin Gaye and Tammy Terrill) made No. 34; Sam Cooke's *Cupid* got to No. 22. Personally, too, Orlando was in turmoil. His sister died; his best friend, actor Freddie Prinze, committed suicide; and he himself was fighting a battle with cocaine. Finally, Orlando had had enough. On stage in Cohasset, Massatusetts, he informed a stunned audience that they were witnessing his last ever live performance, and true to his word, he retired immediately.

He would return, slowly, gingerly, with occasional gigs in Las Vegas, and a 1979 comeback LP, SWEETS FOR MY SWEET. Hopkins went on to star in television's Bosom Buddies with Tom Hanks, Gimme A Break and Family Matters. Vincent joined Smokey Robinson's backing band. And in 1988, Dawn reunited at Trumps in Atlantic City to perform a hit heavy reunion set.

They have reformed several times since then, and of course, their name is invoked every time another hostage situation is satisfactorily resolved. Dawn's greatest achievement, however, is not simply that they gave America one of its most enduring public (as opposed to national ... nobody told people they had to like the song) anthems — It's that through the twenty years, and countless times they have performed the song, they have never looked or sounded sick of it. Orlando himself even compared it to George M.

Cohan's *You're a Grand Old Flag*, but he was still selling himself short. When, after all, was the last time you heard anyone sing, whistle, or even simply grimace, at that?

Discography:

Singles
- *Candida / Look At . . .* (Bell 903, 1970)
- *Knock Three Times / Home* (Bell 938, 1970)
- *I Play And Sing / Get Out From Where We Are* (Bell 970, 1971)
- *Summer Sand / Sweet Soft Sounds Of Love* (Bell 107, 1971)
- *What Are You Doing Sunday / Sweet Soft Sounds Of Love* (Bell 141, 1971)
- *Runaway — Happy Together / Don't Act Like A Baby* (Bell 175, 1972)
- *Vaya Con Dios / I Can't Believe How Much I Love You* (Bell 225, 1972)
- *You're A Lady / In The Park* (Bell 285, 1972)
- *Tie A Yellow Ribbon / I Can't Believe How Much I Love You* (Bell 318, 1973)
- *Say, Has Anybody Seen My Sweet Gypsy Rose / The Spark Of Love* (Bell 375, 1973)
- *Who's In The Strawberry Patch With Sally / Ukelele Man* (Bell 424, 1973)
- *It Only Hurts When I Smile / Sweet Summer Days* (Bell 450, 1974)
- *Steppin' Out / She Can't Hold A Candle To You* (Bell 601, 1974)
- *Look In My Eyes Pretty Woman / My Love Has No Pride* (Bell 620, 1974)
- *Gimme A Good Old Mammy Song / Little Heads In Bunk Beds* (Arista 0105, 1975)
- *Skybird / That's The Way A Wallflower Grows* (Arista 0156, 1975)
- *He Don't Love You / Pick It Up* (Elektra 240, 1975)
- *Mornin' Beautiful / Dance Rosalie Dance* (Elektra 260, 1975)
- *You're All I Need To Get By / Know You Like A Book* (Elektra 275, 1975)
- *Cupid / You're Growin' On Me* (Elektra 302, 1976)
- *Midnight Love Affair / The Selfish Ones* (Elektra 319, 1976)
- *Sing / Sweet On Candy* (Elektra 387, 1977)
- *Growin' On Me / You're All I Need* (Elektra 432, 1977)
- *Bring It On Home To Me / Don't Let Go* (Elektra 501, 1978)
- *I Count The Tears / This Is Rock And Roll* (Elektra 542, 1978)

Albums
- CANDIDA (Bell 6052, 1970)
- DAWN FEATURING TONY ORLANDO (Bell 6069, 1971)
- TUNEWEAVING (Bell 1112, 1973)
- DAWN'S RAGTIME FOLLIES (Bell 1130, 1973)
- PRIME TIME (Bell 1317, 1974)
- GREATEST HITS (Arista 4045, 1975)
- SKYBIRD (Arista 4059, 1975)
- HE DON'T LOVE YOU (Like I Love You) (Elektra 7E 1034, 1975)
- TO BE WITH YOU (Elektra 7E 1049, 1976)

~ 24 ~
The Defranco Family

1973: *Heartbeat, It's A Lovebeat*

By 1973, the family jewels of the Jacksons, the Osmonds and the Partridge Family ruled supreme, but of course they were not alone. On both sides of the Atlantic there was a growing need, primarily among middle-aged record company executives, to create lesser darlings in the hope of grabbing a slice of the teenybop pie.

They were encouraged, oddly enough, by the problem pages in the teen mags. "I don't love Donny / David / Tito any longer," Bereaved of Boston would write in. "Because I don't think he loves me. I wish there was someone else I could adore." Or words to that effect. And in boardrooms across the western world, great minds would unite to help mend Bereaved's broken heart.

For some reason, most of the offenders appeared to be British. The James Boys from East London; Darren Burns, the son of an EMI top dog; Jonathan King protégé Simon Turner; the Poole Family, the Handley Family ... all emerged from the wasteland of Donnymania, cut a few records, struck a few poses, and ultimately succeeded in doing nothing more than turning even more people on to the originals.

Not that America came up with anything better. The Brady Bunch was primal post-Partridge weeny-bait, a widow and widower locked in perpetual sitcom madness with their respective broods and a kindly maid, vindicated only by the cast's failure to record much more than a Christmas album. Then there was Andy and David Williams, nephews of Andy senior, riding on the coat tails of their uncle's credibility (the man who discovered the Osmonds), but still unable to cut much ice with the teenyboppers. They, too, slipped quickly into oblivion, and if there was anybody who could have threatened the Big Three, it was Canadian quintet the DeFranco Family. They, at least, managed a major hit, when *Heartbeat — It's A Lovebeat* went Top 3 in America in 1973.

Naturally, the group's backers singled out the youngest sibling, 13 year old Tony, for attention — the group actually referred to itself as the DeFranco Family Featuring Tony DeFranco, long before most people even knew what a Tony DeFranco was. And naturally, the group radiated sincerity, so much so that it was hard to believe they were a simple pop group. They should have been running a charm school.

But there was an unreal feel to them as well. David Cassidy was the boy-next-door, and he dropped by your house every Monday night to say hello. Donny was less visible, but if you gave up drinking coke, it was at least possible to feel close to him. But what did Tony DeFranco have beyond a pretty face? If the fate of subsequent DeFranco Family (featuring Tony DeFranco) records is anything to go by, not very much.

In America, Cassidy's retirement, the Osmonds' paling and the Jacksons' slow submersion into more mature pastures was to leave a void which would never be satisfactorily filled. Leif Garrett and David's brother Shaun tried their best, but with just four Top 10 hits between them, their best was patently not good enough. If pre-teen enthusiasm was directed anywhere, then, it was towards one of the most unlikely phenomena of the new decade, Scotland's Bay City Rollers, and a string of passing fancies which made the craze-soaked years of 60's hula hoops and twists seem positively anodyne by comparison. There were Wombles from England, there were CBs from the mid-west, and there were martial arts, from the far, Far East.

Discography:
Singles
- *Heartbeat — It's A Lovebeat / Sweet, Sweet Loretta*
  (20th Century Fox 2030, 1973)
- *Abracadabra / Same Kinda Love* (20th Century Fox 2070, 1973)
- *Save The Last Dance For Me / Because We Both Are Young*
  (20th Century Fox 2088, 1974)
- *Write Me A Letter / Baby Blue* (20th Century Fox 2128, 1974)
- *We Belong Together / Time Enough For Love*
  (20th Century Fox 2214, 1975)
Albums
- HEARTBEAT — IT'S A LOVEBEAT (20th Century Fox 422, 1973)
- SAVE THE LAST DANCE FOR ME (20th Century Fox 441, 1974)

~ 25 ~
Carl Douglas

1974: *Kung Fu Fighting*

When the greatest disco records of all time are finally tabulated, Carl Douglas' *Kung Fu Fighting* is a dead certain for inclusion even though it wasn't really a disco record.

When the greatest reggae records of all time are listed, *Kung Fu Fighting* is a shoo in there as well, for, although it was scarcely a reggae record, Douglas was born in Kingston, Jamaica.

And when Robyn Hitchcock's ultimate best of collection is issued, *Kung Fu Fighting* will be included there as well, for even he has not been immune to its charms . . . its infectiousness . . . its almost irresistible majesty.

None of which is at all bad for a record which was spawned by a passing western fancy for all things martial arty, at that odd point in the 1970's when there hadn't had a serious new dance craze in years. Not, mind you, that kung fu was a particularly good theme for a dance craze. With all those flying feet and waving hands, and a volley of vocal sounds which could drown out all but the most stubborn DJ, the only bystanders who got anything at all out of the kung fu dance craze were the ambulance men who encircled the disco, waiting for the casualties to start pouring out. Dance The Kung Fu? — not with two broken legs and a concussion, you won't.

Actor Bruce Lee started it on the cinema screen. David Carradine continued it for network television. But if any name today remains irrevocably tied to the kung fu craze, it was Carl Douglas, a portly, balding, 32 year old who slammed into pop cultural consciousness in the summer of 1974 with three minutes of *Kung Fu Fighting* followed it up with three more of *Dance The Kung Fu*, and then, to all intents and purposes, vanished from sight until 1997 brought an amazing rap revival of his greatest hit, performed by Bus Stop . . . featuring Carl Douglas.

Born in Kingston, raised in California, Douglas arrived in London in his mid-teens, in the 1950's to pursue a Bachelors degree in Mechanical Engineering. Singing, however, was a hobby which became more and more important to him as he grew older, and by the early 1960's, he was fronting the Charmers, a semi-professional R&B band whose specialties included just about anything the audience wanted to hear.

Graduating to the same inner sanctum of London clubs as had already produced stars of the calibre of Cliff Richard and Adam Faith — most notably, the legendary 2 I's coffee house in Old Compton Street — the Charmers were playing a typically tumultuous lunch time set when booking agent John Gunnell, and his songwriter brother Richard, happened to drop by.

Instantly impressed by Douglas, if not the rest of his band, the Gunnells offered to take him under their entrepreneurial wing, waiting while Douglas formed a new band, the Big Stampede, and then launching him into the pulsing heart of swinging London. Nightly, the Marquee, the Flamingo, the Cromwellian, the Bag O'Nails, the creme de la creme of metropolitan clubbery, would get down and sweaty to Douglas' dynamic show. Nightly, too, a host of local and visiting musicians would drop by to jam with them. Ben E King played a memorable set with the Big Stampede, Georgie Fame, Zoot Money . . . and when Chas Chandler first brought a young American guitarist named Jimi Hendrix to London, one of his first stops was wherever the Big Stampede was playing, to allow Hendrix to sample some authentic British soul.

By 1966, too, Herman's Hermits producer Micky Most was watching the Big Stampede's development, although when the band did sign a deal, it was with Go, a newly launched subsidiary of CBS. *Crazy Feeling* (backed by *Keep It To Myself*, by the Peter Perry Soul Band) appeared late in the year, and was voted a resounding smash on British television's much missed pop pundit program, Juke Box Jury. In any event, it didn't chart, but Go still demanded a second single from the band, *Let The Birds Sing / Something For Nothing*. It, too, failed, and when Go Records went under, the Big Stampede followed suit.

Douglas went solo for a short time, cutting a brace of 45's for UA (*Nobody Cries / Serving A Sentence Of Life* and *Sell My Soul To The Devil / Good Hard Worker*.) However, an appearance at the Cannes Film Festival in 1967 saw the singer introduced to Johnny Halliday's backing band, a unit which he promptly hijacked for his own. Combining them with another top rated continental group, a Spanish combo called the Lynx, Douglas renamed them The Explosion, and over the next couple of years, he toured Europe almost exclusively, building up a massive following and apparently scoring a hit single in Spain, with a cover of a (now forgotten) Johnny Taylor song.

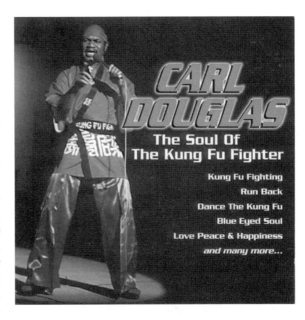

By 1970, however, Douglas was hankering again for success in his adopted homeland, returning to London to join the Gas, a good rocking soul / funk band whose vocalist, Bobby Tench, had just quit to join the Jeff Beck Group. Renaming themselves Gonzales, the band became one of the hot hopes of the new decade, all the more so since Douglas also kept his solo career alive, doubling the band's exposure with near hits like *Do You Need My Love* (CBS, 1971), *Somebody Stop This Madness* (Blue Mountain, 1971) and *Marble And Iron* (US Buddah, 1971.) He also recorded a near-definitive version of Bill Withers' *Lean On Me*, and by the time Gonzales signed with EMI, in 1973, Douglas was widely regarded among the best soul singers working on either side of the Atlantic.

Indian producer Biddu Appian was impressed enough to recruit Douglas to sing the main theme to the 1972 Chuck Connors movie EMBASSY (which Biddu was producing), while the renowned cabaret act, the Dave Davani Sextet regularly invited him to guest with them at the Mayfair Penthouse. Actual chart success, however, continued to keep him at arm's length, a frustration which Douglas and Gonzales bassist Phil Chen began taking out through a course in aikido, held at a hall in Hammersmith, west London. A fascination with other martial arts duly followed, and early in 1974, Douglas wrote a song to celebrate his hobby, a frivolous little ditty called *Kung Fu Fighting*. His bandmates hated it.

The inspiration for the song, Douglas later revealed, was witnessing a fight in a London amusement arcade. Kung Fu was THE in thing, and any young man with even a modicum of physical co-ordination suddenly seemed to fancy himself as a black belt in one Oriental discipline or another. Of course a crowd had gathered to watch as the protagonists hurled themselves at one another, clucking and "eeeeee-iiiiiiii"-ing with gay, grasshopper-esque abandon, and in the midst of the melee, Douglas overheard someone marvel, "everybody is kung fu fighting." And fast as lightning . . .

Douglas filed the song away for future reference, and got on with his life as a hard working soul man. One night at the Mayfair Penthouse, Douglas spotted a woman in the audience who seemed the perfect target for a rude joke he wanted to tell. She was duly shocked; her boyfriend was duly impressed . . . and backstage, he introduced himself to Douglas as visiting American singer Curtis Mayfield, and offered Gonzales the support slot on his upcoming British tour.

Nightly, Mayfield would watch Gonzales' set, and nightly, his own conviction grew. Douglas was wasted in a band. Finally, one night at the London Speakeasy, where Douglas alone was jamming with the Average White Band, Mayfield offered up his considered advice. Go solo. Douglas didn't need telling twice. He quit, shortly before Gonzales began work on their debut album, 1974's GONZALES.

Heading into Nova Studios with Biddu, Douglas decided to launch his latest career twist with *I Want To Give You My Everything*, written by Larry (*Rhinestone Cowboy*) Weiss. It was a fair enough song, appealing in the same way that a lot of soft soul ballads were at that time. But a passing Pye Records scout, Robyn Blanchflower, was less impressed. He thought the proposed B-side, *Kung Fu Fighting* was the stronger song and that despite producer Biddu being so underwhelmed that he'd given Douglas just 15 minutes to record it in. Blanchflower's colleagues at Pye, however, agreed with their talent scout, and in August, 1974, *King Fu Fighting* was unleashed upon an unsuspecting world.

A month later, it was topping charts everywhere, Britain and America included. Sales climbed above ten million and earned Douglas a Grammy for the year's best selling record. An immediate follow up, *Dance The Kung Fu*, won another month on the British chart. An album, KUNG FU FIGHTER, was ready to stuff stockings all over Europe that Christmas.

Unfortunately . . . The problem with scoring such an instantly recognizable, and in all fairness gimmick laden hit, of course, is that nobody expects anything better from the artist or his friends. Even Gonzales, tarred with the brush of their former relationship, were prompted to name their sophomore album MUSIC IS OUR ONLY WEAPON, as though to distance themselves from their old singer's fists of fury.

Douglas himself, however, was heading up a cul de sac from which there could be no redemption. KUNG FU FIGHTER was an excellent album, again in a very mid-70's soft soul kind of way. Biddu's string arrangements, simultaneously lush and explosive, were magnificent, and Douglas' treatment of the (largely self composed) material drew upon all the experience that his decade in clubs and bars had granted him.

But the record did nothing. Even with a jacket photo depicting the singer in full martial drag, KUNG FU FIGHTER was doomed for the remainder bins from the moment it hit the streets, and successive singles ... *Blue Eyed Soul, I Want To Give You My Everything, Love Peace And Happiness, Shanghai'd* . . . were passed over with equal passion. So was a second Douglas album, 1975's LOVE PEACE AND HAPPINESS. So was a third, 1977's KEEP PLEASING ME.

But Douglas did scrape another hit single, when December 1977's *Run Back* made No. 25 in Britain, and though it would be almost exactly 20 years before he again sniffed chart glory ... with the aforementioned Bus Stop revival of his greatest hit ... the sheer cultural intensity of *Kung Fu Fighting* ensures that Carl Douglas will never be forgotten. Overlooked, yes. Underrated, for sure. But forgotten? Never.

Discography:
Singles
- *Crazy Feeling / Keep It To Myself* (Okeh 7268, 1966)
- *Let The Birds Sing / Something For Nothing* (Okeh 7287, 1967)
- *King Fu Fighting / Gamblin' Man* (20th Century Fox 2140, 1974)
- *Dance The Kung Fu / Changing Times* (20th Century Fox 2168, 1975)
- *Blue Eyed Soul* (part one) / *Blue Eyed Soul* (part two)
  (20th Century Fox 2179, 1975)
- *Witch Finder General / Never Had This Dream Before*
  (20th Century Fox 2192, 1976)

Albums
- KUNG FU FIGHTING AND OTHER GREAT LOVE SONGS
  (20th Century Fox T-464, 1974)
- LOVE PEACE AND HAPPINESS (Pye, UK import, 1975)
- KEEP PLEASING ME (Pye, UK import, 1977)

~ 26 ~
ABBA

1974: *Waterloo*

At their peak, they were bigger than the Beatles. In their homeland, they were the biggest export ever. And throughout the decade following their worldwide emergence, as winners of the 1974 Eurovision Song Contest, ABBA's sole goal appeared to be establishing themselves as the most commercially successful pop group of the 1970's. They succeeded with room to spare.

ABBA's roots dated back to the mid-1960's, when vocalist / keyboardist Benny Andersson quit the local Beatles-esque beat group the Hep Stars to join with vocalist Bjorn Ulvaeus, a pairing which swiftly came to the attention of one of the godfathers of the Swedish music scene, Stig Anderson.

Anderson had his first song published in Sweden in 1950, when he was 19 years old, and in 1953, Anderson became Sweden's newest and youngest music publisher, when he unveiled what would become a startlingly successful modus operandi. Picking his material from Radio Luxembourg, the continent's premier popular music station, Anderson would write Swedish language lyrics to the biggest hits of the day, then recruit local musicians to record them for a never ending string of hit singles. 1959's *Klas-G* went gold throughout Scandinavia and the Netherlands. By 1960, Anderson's Sweden Music was handling Scandinavian publishing for most of the major Anglo American houses.

Ulvaeus and Andersson became an integral part of Stig's studio set-up. As the Hootenanny Singers, the duo became the first act to be signed to his Polar Records label. In 1969, Stig joined them in a new publishing venture, Union Songs, and by 1971, Bjorn, Benny and non-performing co-writer Stig had formed a new band with the younger mens' fiancés, Agnetha Faltskog — then still riding the success of her Swedish chart topper *I Was So in Love* — and Frida Lyngstad — Mary Magdalene in the Swedish version of Andrew Lloyd Webber's JESUS CHRIST SUPERSTAR. (the pair married in 1971 and Ulvaeus and Faltskog followed them to the altar in 1978.)

The quartet made their live debut in a Gothenburg nightclub on Valentine's Day, appearing as the Engaged Couples. The performance was a disaster, and plans to continue as a group were abandoned. Stig, however, encouraged them to try again, lending them fresh ambition when, following the 1971 suicide of his business partner, he gave Bjorn and Benny a production partnership within Polar Records. ABBA was officially formed in 1972, in which year Andersson and Ulvaeus won a major hit with *People Need Love*, which featured Faltskog and Lyngstad as backing vocalists.

That same year, Bjorn and Benny's *Better To Have Love* became Sweden's most successful ever entry in the annual Eurovision Song Contest finishing third, and in 1973, with Stig completing an awesome song writing trio, the team submitted another song, *Ring Ring*. This time, they were not so lucky, but they tried again a year later, and of course, they went all the way. *Waterloo* was the runaway winner at the 1974 Contest, and by the end of the year, the song had topped charts all across Europe; made the Top 10 in America, and single-handedly established ABBA as Eurovision's biggest band ever.

Traditionally, few Eurovision victors ever score subsequent hits outside of their homeland, and so it proved with ABBA. *Ring Ring* made No. 32 in Britain (and bombed in America.) *Honey Honey* got to No. 27 in America (but did nothing in Britain), and *So Long* failed to make either chart. But *I Do I Do I Do I Do* returned ABBA to the lower reaches of the British Top 40 in April, 1975, and that summer, the insistent *S.O.S.* reached No. 6. By Christmas, ABBA were back on top, when *Mamma Mia* gave them a second British No. 1.

Fernando, and *Dancing Queen* (ABBA's sole US No. 1) followed, each adding a new dimension to ABBA's burgeoning trademark sound, a blend of sophisticated lushness and buoyant, neo-Bubblegum pop. By the spring of 1976, ABBA was already justified in releasing a first Greatest Hits collection. Within a couple of years, they were halfway towards completing a second.

Their crowning moment came in 1977, first when a staggering 3.5 million people applied for 11,000 tickets to see ABBA play London's Royal Albert Hall. They then released THE ALBUM, their fourth album (and, after GREATEST HITS and ARRIVAL, their third successive British No. 1.) And more than 20 years on, it remains the peak of their achievement. Catching the group with photographic accuracy just as they made that seamless transition from gorgeous pop to Wonderloaf disco, THE ALBUM reveals ABBA as something more than the incessant jukebox of memory; something more, too, than simply a child of the 70's, given new life by the gods of Born Again Kitsch.

The maddeningly insistent *Take A Chance On Me* is the album's killer hit, with *Name Of The Game* a deceptively sultry second. But the opening *Eagle* sets a stage of such unremitting lushness that nothing which follows falls flat. Effortlessly, the Swedish quartet swing from the (surely autobiographical) divorce drama of *One Man, One Woman*, to the supremely buoyant *Hole In Your Soul*, but the crowning moment is the grandiosely titled *The Girl With The Golden Hair — 3 Scenes From A Mini-musical*.

Comprising the hit *Thank You For The Music*, the lilting *I Wonder*, and the Queen-esque ambition of *I'm A Marionette*, what could, in other hands, have seemed an unbearable conceit (three scenes from a mini-musical indeed) becomes an absolute triumph, a sensation which repeated plays of the entire album only enhances.

1978 saw ABBA's star rise even higher with the release of the box office bonanza ABBA-THE MOVIE. It was ironic, then, that as their commercial stock soared, their private relationships plummeted. 1979's VOULEZ VOUS album is an oft-times painful document of marital strife, as Ulvaeus and Faltskog's marriage crumbled. By the time of 1980's SUPER TROUPER, Andersson and Lyngstad, too, had divorced. But whereas other bands, most famously Fleetwood Mac, were able to make monster musical capital out of such disasters, creating their most finely tuned and stylized album ever (1977's RUMOURS), ABBA was not so adept at turning misfortune into fortunes.

The singles *Does Your Mother Know, Angel Eyes, Gimme Gimme Gimme (A Man After Midnight)* and *The Winner Takes All,* beautifully crafted though they were evidenced the group's weakening. They remained great pop, but gone was the instinctive defiance and majesty of those earlier hits.

Gone, too, was the devil-may-care ambition which once marked ABBA out as the logical successors to the Beatles (or, less generously, ELO) in terms of pop classicism. Suddenly the genius sounded strained, as though the team was more intent on being seen to create art, than to simply create it, a process which reached its nadir with the hideous overblown bloat of 1982's THE VISITORS. Finally, ABBA split, Lyngstad and Faltskog heading off for solo careers, Andersson and Ulvaeus for a collaboration with Tim Rice on the musical CHESS. A projected 1986 reunion, to be built around an album called OPUS 10, was canned with just one song completed — *I'm A City.* And that was that.

Having so dominated the 70's and early 80's, however, ABBA's specter could never be laid for good. In 1992, a greatest hits collection, ABBA GOLD went to No. 1 in Britain, even as a collection of the group's Spanish language recordings, ABBA — ORO topped charts throughout the Latin world. Soon after, the British dance duo Erasure released their own tribute to ABBA, the ABBA-ESQUE EP, and found themselves at No. 1, while Australian impersonators Bjorn Again were rewarded with a string of cover hits too.

In 1993, U2 incorporated a version of *Dancing Queen* into their Zoo TV world tour (they were joined on stage by Andersson and Ulvaeus in Stockholm), and as the mid-1990's lurched into a disco revival, ABBA found themselves caught up in that as well. Finally, 1999 saw the wholesale reissue of ABBA's entire catalog, across nine albums, a boxed set of 26 singles, and a new Andersson / Ulvaeus theater project, this time dedicated to the music of ABBA themselves.

Discography:
Singles
 ○ *Waterloo / Watch Out* (Atlantic 3035, 1974)
 ○ *Honey Honey / Dance* (Atlantic 3209, 1974)
 ○ *Hasta Manana / Ring Ring* (Atlantic 3240, 1975)
 ○ *SOS / Man In The Middle* (Atlantic 3265, 1975)
 ○ *I Do I Do I Do / Bang A Boomerang* (Atlantic 3310, 1975)
 ○ *Mamma Mia / Tropical Loveland* (Atlantic 3315, 1976)
 ○ *Fernando / Rock Me* (Atlantic 3346, 1976)
 ○ *Dancing Queen / That's Me* (Atlantic 3372, 1976)
 ○ *Knowing Me Knowing You / Happy Hawaii* (Atlantic 3387, 1977)
 ○ *Money Money Money / Crazy World* (Atlantic 3434, 1977)
 ○ *The Name Of The Game / I Wonder* (Atlantic 3449, 1977)
 ○ *Take A Chance On Me / I'm A Marionette* (Atlantic 3457, 1978)
 ○ *Does Your Mother Know / Kisses Of Fire* (Atlantic 3574, 1979)

- ○ *Voulez Vous / Angeleyes* (Atlantic 3609, 1979)
- ○ *Chiquitita / Lovelight* (Atlantic 3629, 1979)
- ○ *Gimme Gimme Gimme A Man After Midnight / The King Has Lost His Crown* (Atlantic 3652, 1980)
- ○ *The Winner Takes It All / Elaine* (Atlantic 3776, 1980)
- ○ *Super Trouper / The Piper* (Atlantic 3806, 1981)
- ○ *On And On And On / Lay All Your Love On Me* (Atlantic 3826, 1981)
- ○ *When All Is Said And Done / Should I Laugh Or Cry* (Atlantic 3889, 1982)
- ○ *The Visitors / Head Over Heels* (Atlantic 4031, 1982)
- ○ *The Day Before You Came / Cassandra* (Atlantic 89948, 1982)
- ○ *One Of Us / Should I Laugh Or Cry* (Atlantic 89881, 1983)

Albums
- ○ WATERLOO (Atlantic 18101, 1974)
- ○ ABBA (Atlantic 18146, 1975)
- ○ GREATEST HITS (Atlantic 18189, 1976)
- ○ ARRIVAL (Atlantic 18207, 1977)
- ○ THE ALBUM (Atlantic 19164, 1978)
- ○ VOULEZ VOUS (Atlantic 16000, 1979)
- ○ GREATEST HITS VOL 2 (Atlantic 16009, 1979)
- ○ SUPER TROUPER (Atlantic 16023, 1980)
- ○ THE VISITORS (Atlantic 19332, 1981)
- ○ LIVE (Atlantic 81675, 1986)

~ 27 ~
The Bay City Rollers

1975: *Saturday Night*

Many groups attempted to blast into the teen idol stakes as the 1970's progressed, and the familymania of earlier years began to recede. In terms of combining success, great songs and a cohesive image, however, none could rival the Bay City Rollers. For two years in Britain, and a little less in America, the Rollers' tartan uniform and lavatory brush haircuts were a sartorial staple which no self-respecting obsessive could be without, while all that the Osmonds did for Mormon, the Rollers did for Scotland. From the English south-east to the American northwest, Scots accents were suddenly THE height of fashion, and if the majority of these rolling brogues and intonations simply sounded silly, still the Rollers were the first band since the Beatles to provoke such a rash of linguistic acrobatics. And that has to count for something.

Astutely managed by one Tam Paton, the Rollers had been around in various forms since 1968, plugging their way around the ballrooms of Scotland and the north even after a meeting with pop svengali Jonathan King gifted them with their first hit single, a cover of the Gentrys' 1965 US smash *Keep On Dancing*.

King already visualized the band as a teenybop phenomenon, a fate thwarted only by his self-confessed inability to follow up that initial breakthrough. "I'm probably stronger than most people on the actual grooves of a record, and for that reason I come through with more first time hits than most people. But likewise, I'm less good at following it."

As it was, it was to take the Rollers another two and a half years, two changes of producer and any number of personnel changes, before they were to see any further reward for their labors. By the time *Remember (Sha La la)* gave them a Top Ten hit in June, 1974, it's unlikely that anyone who even remembered *Keep On Dancing* would have actually recognized the new line-up; only Alan and Derek Longmuir, the band's elderly rhythm section, remained from the *Keep On Dancing* combo. They were joined now by guitarist Stuart "Woody" Wood and vocalist Les McKeown. Lead guitarist Eric Faulkner followed, shortly after the release of *Remember*. Tam Paton would occasionally add piano (it later transpired that this line up was, in fact, purely theoretical. In 1975 Paton confessed that the band had not played on any of their records prior to their chart-topping reworking of the Four Seasons' *Bye Bye Baby*.)

The Rollers now recorded under the aegis of Bill Martin and Phil Coulter, veterans of countless British campaigns through the trenches of the annual Eurovision Song Contest, and it must be admitted that *Remember*, the principle lyric of which was the subtitled "Sha la la," was hardly as awesome an achievement as its Top Ten predecessor. Also, like King, the pair were not renowned for following up their successes in particularly convincing style. But with a genius few people ever gave him credit for, Tam Paton had finally come upon a solution.

When the Rollers appeared on television to promote *Keep On Dancing*, that was all they had been doing, promoting a record. They were simply a group playing a song. There was no image, no point of reference, nothing to make any young, impressionable mind latch onto the band and want to emulate it. And that, in an increasingly image-conscious teenaged market, was a dangerous omission.

This time around, Paton was adamant that his boys should be instantly identifiable, kitting them out with a tartan uniform which was destined to become the fashion accessory of 1975.

The outfit itself was modeled around the skinhead image that had swept Britain around 1970-71 — the long-sleeved shirts and braces, rolled up trouser bottoms and big boots which once sent fear shooting through the soul of anyone unfortunate enough to come across a gang of young folk dressed like that. The Rollers softened the look, however. They replaced denim with tartan, DMs with platforms, and let the spikey hair grow to Persian cat proportions. Threat became theater, imminent violence became unbridled love, and a nowhere bunch of Scots bar musicians became superstars in waiting.

Remember was followed into the chart by *Shang-A-Lang*, a masterpiece of fluff which found its insidious way into every heart which heard it, whether they would admit it or not. Six years later, latter-day Roller Ian Mitchell was still performing it live, clad in gymslip, fishnet stockings and fur stole. "And why not?," he'd growl if you asked him why. "It's a great song."

It was with *Shang-A-Lang*, which reached number two in April, 1974, that the phenomenon which became Rollermania was first sighted on the streets of Great Britain, platoons of hard-faced Rollergirls stalking the streets in their immaculate tartan uniforms and daring anybody to denigrate their heroes. Within a year the platoon had become an army, united in their love of the Rollers and apparent hatred for the rest of humanity. When visiting Americans Milk'n'Cookies insulted the band on the radio, their manager insists the ensuing furor drove them out of the country. When London glitter devils Hello performed a similar faux pas, their manager claims they weren't forgiven until they took out a full page advertisement in one of the pop papers to apologize.

Beginning that spring of 1974, fan loyalties had never been so divided as they were over the next twelve months or so. Supporters of the Osbros and Cassidy had at least regarded one another with a mutual respect, tempers flaring only when the subject of looks came about. Rollergirls, however, had no time for any of that. They would fight, to the death if necessary, for the honor of the adored objects. Even internal warfare was not beyond the reach of their loyalty. When the Rollers played the seaside town of Bournemouth, full scale fights broke out as Woody's Wonders did battle with Les' Lovelies, and the Ladies bathroom was a scene of unremitting chaos as stewards tried to deal with the tidal wave of boys breaking in through the window to discover why their womenfolk had suddenly gone haywire. And everywhere you went that summer, *Summerlove Sensation*, the Rollers' finest hour by far, was to be heard drifting out of beach transistors and fairground Wurlitzers all season long.

Rollermania reached its peak the following spring with the group's surprisingly innovative reworking of the Four Seasons' *Bye Bye Baby*. It gave them their first number one, and the nationwide tour which accompanied it was given rapturous support by a media which had finally awoken to the fact that a British act was finally challenging the Americans' stranglehold on local youth affections.

"Roll over Donny, tell David the news, the Rollers are coming for You, You and YOU!" was one of the more innovative headlines, set in inch thick capitals over a grainy picture of the Rollers' latest in-concert triumph.

It mattered not that the band was of only average musical ability, nor that not one of them was even remotely great looking. The fact that the band had inspired this kind of support without the aid of any but the most blatant pin-up oriented magazines, suggested that the Rollers were more than a teenage fad, they were the REAL THING.

Maisy, a 16 year old Scottish girl, explained to Record Mirror magazine how she felt about her particular favorite, Eric: "He's my dream come true, my god. I thought it was just a fad, but now I've really grown to love him deeply. My parents think I'm crazy and the teachers at school have lectured me about my failed exams, and the way my standard of work has dropped since I became a Rollers' fan. They just cannot begin to understand that Eric is the most important thing to me."

The Rollers were not adverse to taking advantage of this kind of thing. "Before I joined the Rollers I used to have my fair share of birds running after me," Les once said, "But it wasn't like it is now . . ."

The Bay City Rollers

Only partially veiled tales of on-the-road debauchery grew up around the band, while their off-stage behavior, too, was beginning to cause some very serious concern. Feted as gods, the band tried to act like gods. Les confessed to a sexual proclivity quite unbecoming in a person of his stature, and was then involved in a headline grabbing manslaughter case after he knocked down and killed a senior citizen on a crosswalk.

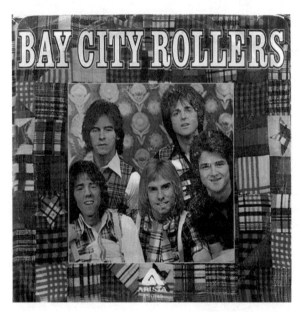

It was to escape the growing pressures that the Rollers, at the height of their British success, set out for America where *Saturday Night* had already given them a No, I hit. Leaving Britain only with memories of their networked TV series Shang-A-Lang, they hit America in the fall of 1975, and found the PR men already priming the publicity pump.

And as their stock rose in the US, it started to dip in their homeland. British fans felt that they'd been deserted by the Rollers. Wasn't their love strong enough to keep the boys at home? From a period of maximum visibility the band were apparent now only in the pages of those newspapers who had bothered briefing their Stateside correspondents to cover some aspect of the outing, and they, too, grew progressively thinner on the ground as the band's absence grew longer and longer.

Of course it was the classic scenario. Only David Bowie, whose very career was built around his invisibility, was to survive lengthy sojourns away from the British public eye. Bolan, Slade and the Sweet, on the other hand, lost any amount of local credibility — and popularity — when they headed across the Atlantic for anything more than the briefest of tours. And while it might also be said that the quality of those bands' record releases declined, primarily as a result of their attempting to gear their music more towards the American listener (and failing!), even the weakest Bolan boogie would still have succeeded had the star only been at home to plug it.

Tam Paton's solution to the Rollers' delinquency was to announce that Alan Longmuir, at 26 the oldest in the group, had quit. In reality, he had been sacked, sacrificed to the band's need to recreate the frenzy of adoration they were so close to losing. His replacement was a 17 year old Belfast boy, Ian Mitchell, upon whom Paton had been keeping tabs for some time. At the time of McKeown's manslaughter charge, Mitchell had been poised to step into his tartan trim booties in the event of the singer being jailed. When Les got off with a simple fine, Ian went back on ice until Alan was ousted.

"I'll never regret having been in the Rollers," says Mitchell, "even though it was totally insane. I was a complete wreck. I was doing speed simply to keep alive. We'd get out at the airport and really, we didn't know if we were going for a shit or a shave." He lasted the pace for just one album, two singles and seven months. "My sanity was at stake. I had to get out before I put my head in the gas oven."

Ian was replaced by another unknown, Pat McGlynn, before Alan returned to the fold when it became apparent that the hysteria of yesteryear would never be recreated, and that the band had better start concentrating on its music if it was ever to survive. When Les McKeown was finally sacked, in November 1978, his passing rated barely a mention in the Anglo-American press, although in Japan and the far East, the fans went so far as to threaten suicide unless he was reinstated. He wasn't, and to the best of anyone's knowledge, the fans didn't.

Today it seems hard to believe that the Rollers' reign lasted little more than a year on either side of the Atlantic. Indeed, America tired of them in considerably less time than that, and that despite being courted not with the bubblegum delights which were the lot of British audiences, but rather with a string of singles which evinced a maturity few British listeners could ever have suspected the Rollers of possessing.

Political in-fighting, chiefly concerned with the band's desire to pen their own B-sides, led to a divorce from the Martin-Coulter team, and the DEDICATION album in particular saw the Rollers' choice of material include the likes of Tim Moore's *Rock'n'Roll Love Letter*, the Dusty Springfield classic *I Only Wanna be With You* and, with a self-deprecating humor a thousand miles removed from the po-faced superiority of old, Vanda / Young's *Yesterday's Heroes*, a song whose message was only compounded by the snatch of prerecorded Rollermania which preceded it.

In personal terms, too, the Rollers were looking shaky. Says Mitchell, "Eric, who was writing most of the songs, wanted more security than he actually had. We split the money five ways, but Eric wanted his full royalty rate on all his songs, and he was shouting about that."

Mitchell continues, "Les was going totally against the image, screwing anything that moved and there were a lot of upheavals regarding Tam. Everyone was arguing and fighting and kicking each other in the head, stabbing each other in the back just to get an inch. And all of us realized the era of the Rollers was coming to an end."

With the death of the Rollers as a marketable commodity came the death of the Teenybop Idol. Although Bell Records had a brave stab at resurrecting the hysteria with Glaswegians Slik, the band itself was never convincing enough in their roles as sex objects for a generation.

Other labels had other bands: Flintlock made something of a splash towards the end of the 70's, but only in terms of their adolescent good looks, blasted into every home by the presence of one member in a television drama series, another in a musicians' workshop type program.

Child scavenged a minor hit, Micky Most scraped together a few more on the back of sundry bouncing boppers, but not until the early eighties' dawn of Duran Duran, Spandau Ballet and Wham! were the kids ever to have something real to scream about. And besides, new musical forces were at work in the mid-1970's, forces which would within months strike a body blow at the marketing concepts which could create such monsters in the first place. Thus Slik (whose greatest claim to fame today lies in giving Midge Ure something to squirm about every time their name comes up in conversation), Child, Flintlock and a host of others died almost before they were born, replaced in the hierarchy of commerce by punk rock, a concern which was no less manufactured than any of its predecessors, but which at least admitted what it was after. Teenage pocket money is a powerful drug.

Discography:
Singles
- ○ *Keep On Dancing / Alright* (Bell 169, 1971)
- ○ *Bye Bye Baby / It's For You* (Arista 0120, 1975)
- ○ *Give A Little Love / She'll Be Crying Over You* (Arista 10883, 1975)
- ○ *Saturday Night / Marlena* (Arista 0149, 1975)
- ○ *Money Honey / Mary Anne* (Arista 0170, 1975)
- ○ *Rock'n'Roll Love Letter / Shanghied In Love* (Arista 0185, 1976)
- ○ *Don't Stop The Music* (disco) */ Don't Stop The Music* (Arista 0193, 1976)
- ○ *I Only Wanna Be With You / Write A Letter* (Arista 0205, 1976)
- ○ *Yesterday's Hero / My Lisa* (Arista 0216, 1977)
- ○ *Dedication / Rock'n'Roller* (Arista 0233, 1977)
- ○ *It's A Game /* (Arista 108, 1977)
- ○ *You Made Me Believe In Magic / Dance Dance Dance* (Arista 256, 1977)
- ○ *The Way I Feel Tonight / Love Power* (Arista 272, 1977)
- ○ *Where Will I Be Now? / If You Were My Woman* (Arista 383, 1978)
- ○ *Turn On The Radio / Hello And Welcome Home* (Arista 476, 1979)

Albums
- ○ BAY CITY ROLLERS (Bell 4049, 1974)
- ○ ROCK'N'ROLL LOVE LETTER (Arista 4071, 1976)
- ○ DEDICATION (Arista 4093, 1976)
- ○ GREATEST HITS (Arista 4158, 1977)
- ○ IT'S A GAME (Arista 7004, 1977)
- ○ STRANGERS IN THE WIND (Arista 4194, 1978)
- ○ ELEVATOR (Arista 4241, 1979)

~ 28 ~
John Travolta

1976: *Let Her In*

Singing actors have always been an occupational hazard in the music business. Indeed, there was a time when you could barely turn around without encountering another thespian superstar with too much time on his or her hands, ensconced in a studio and dutifully massacring another innocent standard. Few, however, were so masterfully produced, and productively masterminded, as the twelve months or so which John Travolta spent as a pop superstar in his own dynamic right.

Between 1976 and 1978, Travolta landed two albums and one compilation into the US Top 200. He scored a Top 10 single and two Top 40 follow ups, and that's without even considering the singing, dancing, streak of hits which accompanied the 1978 movie GREASE — the joyously idiotic *You're The One That I Want*, *Summer Nights*, *Greased Lightning*, and *Sandy*. Indeed, though Travolta today fervently dismisses his musical career as simply a "by product" of his acting career, neither Billboard nor Record World & Music Retail were quite so cynical. Both ended 1976 by awarding him the title of New Pop Male Vocalist of the Year.

"I was a Broadway performer and I know how to sing and I've done recordings," Travolta explained. "I love singing. I'll always love singing. I sing for myself all the time outside the shower. I'm very proud of the successes I've had as a singer. But they were usually, other than one or two, songs correlated to a movie that I was in. My primary career is in acting. So I never took my singing on the same level as acting."

Travolta's early musical career follows that same, unimpeachable, logic. Shortly after his singing voice was heard for the first time, in 1974's OVER HERE stage show, Travolta went into the studio with producers John Reno and John Davis to record a handful of songs. The results were not especially spectacular. Travolta's voice rarely gelled with the distinctly average middle-of-the-road material and arrangements he was offered, and the resultant tapes were shelved.

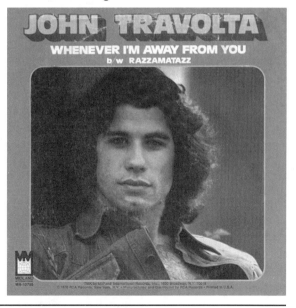

John Travolta

In February, 1976, however, Reno's Midland International label, hot off a handful of massive hits by Silver Convention and Carol Douglas, had picked up Travolta for a solo career. It was a no-lose situation. Despite being so suddenly launched onto precisely the same campaign trail as David Cassidy before him, and David (Starsky and Hutch) Soul shortly after, so far as Midland International was concerned, Travolta represented one of the healthiest investments around.

Blending the 1974 sessions with newer material, the JOHN TRAVOLTA album emerged in March, 1976, as a warm-hearted collection of lightweight ballads and mock-rockers: Eric Carmen's *Never Gonna Fall In Love Again*, Neil Sedaka's *I Don't Know What I Like About You, Baby*, George Benson's *Let Her In*, and so on. And in a way, that was its downfall — as a listening experience, if not as a marketable item. The record, of course, sold like hot-cakes, but the charts only tell you how many people took it home. They don't mention how often the record was played once they got it there.

JOHN TRAVOLTA was pure easy listening, and though Travolta, like so many TV teen idols before and since, doubtless made the album with the best intentions and highest hopes, still the overall impression was of a certain facelessness. The album said a lot about what Travolta's producer and record company wanted him to sound like. The question that it didn't address was what did Travolta himself want to sound like?

Travolta admitted as much when he confessed that though his favorite singer was Barbra Streisand, and Joe Cocker's *You Are So Beautiful* was his personal favorite hit the previous year, still "I don't like contemporary music that well." He conceded that country and western was sometimes "interesting," and he professed a fondness for the Latino sounds of Sergio Mendes. But "my taste is not a set thing. Whatever appeals to me at the time."

Despite his own apparent uncertainty; despite, too, the album's own general mundanity, JOHN TRAVOLTA cracked the American Top 40 in May, 1976, just as Travolta's first single, *Let Her In*, commenced its rise into the Top 10, riding on the same wave of adulation which was simultaneously propelling his TV show's theme music, John Sebastian's *Welcome Back*, to No. 1. Resplendent in a neat crimson sweater, Travolta celebrated with an appearance on American Bandstand, the first of two appearances he made on the show.

Through the summer of 1976, while "Kotter" took its between seasons break, Travolta toured the east coast with a stage show of BUS STOP. However, he later admitted, "when the record albums came out, I was really pressured to do personal appearance tours, promoting them." The money on offer was fabulous as well, up in the region of $25,000 per appearance, and finally, Travolta relented, acceding to a handful of very carefully orchestrated personal appearances.

He apparently hated them, but the results were predictably chaotic. In Cleveland, over 5,000 fans mobbed him. In Schaumburg, Illinois, visiting what was then the world's biggest shopping mall, an estimated 30,000 people turned out to catch a glimpse of their idol. When he visited a mall in New Jersey, 2,000 copies of the album were sold in an hour. Another appearance, in a Long Island department store, drew a crowd of 10,000 and became so wild that Travolta had to be whisked away disguised as a policeman. In June, Midland International took out a full page advertisement in Billboard magazine, simply to trumpet these triumphs to the world.

"New York's been sold! L.A.'s been sold! The Travolta phenomenon has taken the nation by storm! In Chicago, over 25,000 cheering fans packed parking lots just to catch a glimpse of their new-found hero." The ad claimed sales of over 100,000 copies for the album in just two weeks, with *Let Her In* selling even stronger.

Coinciding with the return of Welcome Back Kotter, Midland International released John's second single, *Whenever I'm Away From You*. It would not prove as big a hit as its predecessor, clambering no higher up the chart than No. 38, but still John had made enough of an impression that the New Pop Male Vocalist of the Year awards were his for the taking. Even more perversely, when Robert Stigwood first settled upon Travolta as the star for the forthcoming SATURDAY NIGHT FEVER movie, it was not the young man's acting which impressed him. It was *Let Her In*.

"If I hadn't done that record, my career would have been much different," John laughed years later. He had recently been written up in Time magazine, a portrait of the young man with the No. 3 song in the country, and the No. 1 comedy show. Stigwood and his partner, Allan Carr, read the article . . . and the rest made history.

As 1977 picked up speed, Travolta scored his third, albeit minor, hit single. *All Strung Out On You*, which made No. 34 in February, 1977, had been recorded late in 1976 during a series of sessions with producer Jeff Barry. CAN'T LET YOU GO, an album bringing together another eight of Barry's productions, followed. Another unadventurous collection of ballads, it was most notable for John's reading of Peter Allen's *Back Doors Crying*, a smokey, melancholy song which suggested that Travolta had musical capabilities which far exceeded the limited ambition evinced elsewhere on the album.

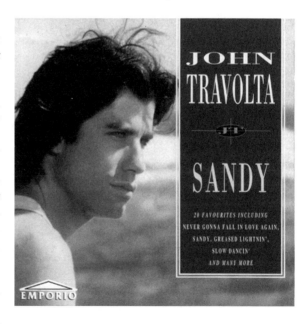

But CAN'T LET YOU GO rose no higher than No. 66. Suggestions that John might record his next album with Carly Simon petered out, and while 1978 did bring a faintly lackluster cover of Jennifer Warnes' *The Right Time Of The Night*, Travolta would never resurrect his singing career. His final release, the nearest thing to a new album which Midland could muster, was a repackaging of the two existing albums under the significantly unimaginative title of TRAVOLTA FEVER. Released in time for Christmas, it stalled at No. 161.

For Travolta, coming off the staggering critical (and commercial) failure of his most recent movie, MOMENT BY MOMENT, it was the final straw. Distancing himself even from the musical movie roles which had done so much to establish him in the first place, Travolta made just one more record, a duet with Olivia Newton John on the soundtrack of 1983's TWO OF A KIND. Then he went back to making movies. At least there, he knew what he was doing.

Discography:
Singles
- *Let Her In / Big Trouble* (Midland International 10623, 1976)
- *Whenever I'm Away From You / Razzamatazz* (Midland International 10780, 1976)
- *All Strung Out On You / Easy Evil* (Midland International 10907, 1977)
- *Slow Dancing /* (Midland International 10997, 1977)
- *Razzamatazz /* (Midland International 11206, 1978)
- *You're The One That I Want* (with Olivia Newton John) /
  Alone at A Drive In Movie (RSO 891, 1978)
- *Summer Nights* (with Olivia Newton John) / *Rock'n'Roll Party Queen*
  (RSO 906, 1978)
- *Greased Lightning* (with Jeff Conaway) / (RSO 909, 1978)
- *Sandy / Blue Moon* (RSO 930, 1978)
- *Twist Of Fate* (with Olivia Newton John) / *Take A Chance*
  (MCA 52284, 1983)

Albums
- JOHN TRAVOLTA (Midland International 1563, 1976)
- CAN'T LET YOU GO (Midland International 2211, 1977)
- TRAVOLTA FEVER (Midland International 001, 1978)

~ 29 ~
New Edition

1983: *Candy Girl*

When producer Maurice Starr first envisioned New Edition in the early 1980's, there was simply no way he could have imagined quite what he was about to unleash — the first all-new black American singing phenomenon since the Jackson Five (the comparisons began even before the hits started rolling) ... one of the most influential R&B acts of the decade ... Bobby Brown ... In the simplest terms, he created a monster, and recreated a scream scene which the country had been trying to rediscover for years.

Boston based New Edition, as their name suggested, were young — at the time of their first record, Bobby Brown, Ralph Tresvant, Ricky Bell, Mike Bivins, and Ronald Davoe were all aged between 13 and 15, and for all the subsequent glory heaped on their heads, it must be admitted that their first smash, 1983's British chart topper, *Candy Girl*, scored as much on the novelty of the quintet's youth, as on the strength of their performance. Indeed, coming at a time when the success of the post-THRILLER Michael Jackson was reacquainting the world with a string of old Jackson Five hits and TV performances, New Edition slipped so thoroughly into the surrogate shoes that *Candy Girl* itself was almost Five by proxy.

New Edition, however, was made of considerably sterner stuff than the Jacko-comparisons immediately assumed. A relatively lightweight pop-packed debut album, titled after that debut hit, was a surprising stiff — it peaked at No. 90 in the US. *Candy Girl* itself made a mere No. 46. A second single, *Is This The End*, reached No. 85. But whereas the band's British fame dissipated almost immediately the last notes of *Candy Girl* faded from earshot, America was simply holding out for something more substantial.

That came with the band's self-titled second album, in the fall of 1984, and a Top 5 single, *Cool It Now* (*Mr. Telephone Man*, an even more memorable song, made No. 12.) A warm concoction built around the smoothest ballads you've ever heard, interspersed with a foot-tapping soupcon of mild Funk Lite, NEW EDITION established its makers as stars, with super stardom not far behind. No matter that ALL FOR LOVE, the group's third album, mustered nothing better than a disappointing No. 32, nor that its attendant singles struggled to do any better, when Bobby Brown left the band shortly after its release, genuine shock waves went through the business.

Certainly, New Edition seemed set to struggle on without him. As both the focal and vocal point of New Edition, the then 17 year old Brown's absence was harshly felt throughout the group's next album, the somewhat desperate UNDER THE BLUE MOON collection of 50's & 60's covers. Of course there was no doubting the quality of songs like *Duke Of Earl*, *Blue Moon*, *Hey There Lonely Girl* and *Tears On My Pillow*. Nor could New Edition's performance be faulted — the quartet turned in harmonies sweeter than any they had  preciously delivered. But that simply wasn't enough. New Edition was important because they spoke to, and of, a musical milieu which had been left voiceless for too long. No matter that the most important message the group's first two albums left was on their girlfriend's answer-phone late at night. New Edition presented their audience with identity and ambition. Now here they were subverting both beneath the kind of record which any sweet singing vocal group could make . . . and which too many had already made, at various points over the last 30 years. UNDER THE BLUE MOON got to No. 43, and New Edition returned to the drawing board.

They re-emerged two years later, older, wilder, wiser and with (at last) a fitting replacement for Brown, Johnny Gill. Close to a decade older than the man he was replacing, DC native Gill already had a fine soul record behind him, most notably in tandem with singer Stacy Lattishaw. Now he would lead New Edition through what would prove to be both their best, and their last, ever album, 1988's HEART BREAK (and the Top 10 hit *If It Isn't Love.*)

The group's break up in 1989 was inevitable. So was the individual members' continued, if less pronounced, success on their own. Gill and Tresvant followed in Bobby Brown's footsteps as solo acts. Bell, Bivins and Devoe remained together in the cleverly named Bell Biv Devoe.

In total, New Edition's reign last for six years. In actuality, their rule was barely six months. The group's importance cannot, however, be gauged purely from chart statistics and theater bookings. All the customary apparatus of pop stardom, in fact, goes out of the window, as New Edition are revealed first, as genuine pioneers of the urban pop sound which would dominate so much of the decade to come, and second, as the testing ground for a whole new Maurice Starr projection, the all-singing, all-dancing, New Kids On The Block.

Discography:
Singles
  ◦ *Candy Girl* / (sing-along version) (StreetWise 1108, 1983)
  ◦ *Is This The End* / (same) (StreetWise 1111, 1983)
  ◦ *Popcorn Girl* / *Jealous Girl* (StreetWise 1116, 1983)
  ◦ *Cool It Now* / (sing-along version) (MCA 52455, 1984)
  ◦ *Mr. Telephone Man* / (instrumental) (MCA 52484, 1984)
  ◦ *Lost In Love* / *Gold Mine* (MCA 52553, 1985)
  ◦ *Kinda Girls We Like* / (album version) (MCA 23544, 1985)
  ◦ *My Secret* / *I'm Leaving You Again* (MCA 52627, 1985)
  ◦ *Count Me Out* / *Good Boys* (MCA 52703, 1985)
  ◦ *A Little Bit Of Love* / *Sneakin' Around* (MCA 52768, 1986)
  ◦ *With You All The Way* / *All For Love* (MCA 52829, 1986)
  ◦ *Earth Angel* / *With You All The Way* (MCA 52905, 1986)
  ◦ *Once In A Lifetime Groove* / (á capella version) (MCA 52959, 1986)
  ◦ *Tears on My Pillow* / *Bring Back The Memories* (MCA 53019, 1987)
  ◦ *Helplessly In Love* / (instrumental) (MCA 53164, 1987)
  ◦ *If It Isn't Love* / (instrumental) (MCA 53264, 1988)
  ◦ *You're Not My Kind Of Girl* / (instrumental) (MCA 53405, 1988)
  ◦ *Can You Stand The Rain* / (instrumental) (MCA 53464, 1989)
  ◦ *Crucial* / (instrumental) (MCA 53500, 1989)
  ◦ *NE Heart Break* / (instrumental) (MCA 53391, 1989)

- *Hit Me Off* / (instrumental) (MCA 55210, 1996)
- *I'm Still In Love With You / You Don't Have To Worry* (MCA 55264, 1996)
- *One More Day / Something About You* (remix) (MCA 55350, 1997)

Albums

- CANDY GIRL (StreetWise 3301, 1983)
- NEW EDITION (MCA 5515, 1984)
- ALL FOR LOVE (MCA 5679, 1985)
- CHRISTMAS ALL OVER THE WORLD (MCA 4987, 1985)
- UNDER THE BLUE MOON (MCA 5912, 1986)
- HEART BREAK (MCA 42207, 1988)
- GREATEST HITS VOLUME ONE (MCA 10434, 1991)
- HOME AGAIN (MCA 11480, 1996)

~ 30 ~
New Kids On The Block

1988: *You Got It (The Right Stuff)*

If anybody ever mistook New Kids On The Block for nothing more than a white and watery version of New Edition, their confusion was easy to understand. Created, again, by Maurice Starr, with the emphasis even more on the creation this time, New Kids On The Block was essentially an object lesson in Learning From One's Mistakes.

Again drawn from the ranks of Boston youth, New Kids On The Block lined up as teens Donnie Wahlberg, Jordan Knight, Jon Knight, Danny Wood and Joe McIntyre, and like New Edition, the all-vocal group spent much of their self-titled debut album struggling to find their feet, musically, commercially, and in terms of a viable image. And once the first was achieved through regular live and television work, the remainder simply followed with almost predictable ease. By the time the Kids' second album, 1988's HANGIN' TOUGH, was on the streets, the funky title track was already a No. 1 smash, *I'll Be Loving You (Forever)* was set to join it, and *You Got It (The Right Stuff)* was destined for the Top 3.

The group's debut album was reissued and made the Top 30. They even recorded a Christmas album, reviving a stunt which had lain all but untouched since the days of the Brady Bunch, Partridge Family et al, and made the Top 10 with it. Indeed, by the end of 1989, New Kidmania was responsible for selling some 13 million copies of the three available albums (HANGIN' TOUGH alone did eight million), and who knows how many magazines, videos, books and baloney.

Young, good looking, kinda tough, the New Kids were a phenomenon aimed unequivocally at the heart of teenaged America (interestingly, it would be several years more before Europe fell for them, and even then the success was short lived.) And

teenaged America swallowed them whole. But as early as 1990, some kind of rot was seeping into view. STEP BY STEP, the group's massively anticipated and hugely promoted third album, made No. 1, but clocked up sales almost one third that of its predecessor. And while the title track, too, was a No. 1, its follow-up climbed no higher than No. 7, as the New Kids succumbed to what must be one of the most ironic fates in pop history, strangled to death by the exact same phenomenon which their erstwhile fellows in the Maurice Starr stable, New Edition, had helped to kick start, the melodic urban balladry which now existed on the fringes of the harder rap scene. Just as so many teen idols had discovered in the distant pop past, even teen idols' audiences have to grow up. The difference was, the New Kids' grew up at light speed.

An ill-judged attempt to redesign themselves as NKOTB proved less than successful, and the group signed off with NO MORE GAMES — THE REMIX ALBUM, a smartly done, but ultimately soulless attempt to breathe new life into a string of greatest hits which had lasted less than two years. Four years later, without Starr at the helm, they even released a new album, a brave urban set called, somewhat fittingly, FACE THE MUSIC. It failed, and the group packed it all in. And while it would be another four years before a viable American replacement came along, in the form of Florida's Backstreet Boys, over the ocean in Europe the teen dream scheme was undergoing a major revival all its own.

Discography:
Singles
- Be My Girl / (instrumental) (Columbia 05883, 1986)
- Please Don't Go Girl / Whatcha Gonna Do About It (Columbia 07700, 1988)
- You Got It / (long version) (Columbia 08092, 1988)
- I'll Be Loving You (Forever) / (instrumental) (Columbia 68671, 1989)
- Hangin' Tough / Didn't I Blow Your Mind (Columbia 68960, 1989)
- Cover Girl / Merry Merry Christmas (Columbia 69088, 1989)
- This One's For The Children / Funky Funky Xmas (Columbia 73064, 1989)
- Step By Step / Valentine Girl (Columbia 73343, 1990)
- Let's Try It Again / Popsicle (Columbia 73443, 1990)
Albums
- NEW KIDS ON THE BLOCK (Columbia 40475, 1987)
- HANGIN' TOUGH (Columbia 40985, 1988)
- MERRY MERRY CHRISTMAS (Columbia 45280, 1989)
- STEP BY STEP (Columbia 45129, 1990)
- NO MORE GAMES — THE REMIX ALBUM (Columbia 46959, 1990)

NKOTB
Singles
   ○ *If You Go Away / Games* (the Kids Get Hard mix) (Columbia 74255, 1992)
   ○ *Dirty Dawg /* (remix) (Columbia 77293, 1994)
Albums
   ○ FACE THE MUSIC (Columbia 52969, 1994)

~ 31 ~
Milli Vanilli

1989: *Baby Don't Forget My Number*

It was, a scandalized media insisted, the sensation of the decade. It was, fumed Variety, the "biggest disgrace in Grammy history." Grammy winners Milli Vanilli stripped of the honor they so richly deserved, Best New Artist of 1989, because — horror of unprecedented horrors — they didn't actually play, sing or anything, on the record that bore their name. No, they were simply the pretty boy front men for an otherwise faceless dance crew created by German pop maestro Frank Farian — the man who gave us Boney M and the Far Corporation and who, therefore, knew precisely what he was doing. Which was creating magnificent mindless dance music for the masses. Nothing more, nothing less.

It wasn't his fault that the Grammy committee looked out over a landscape packed with the emergent talents of Neneh Cherry, Soul II Soul, the Indigo Girls and Tone Loc (the year's other nominees) and decided that Milli Vanilli were better than any of them. It wasn't Milli Vanilli's fault, either. They played along with the goof because that's what it was, the already artificial honor of a Grammy going to the ultimate in artifice — at least since the Monkees landed two nominations in 1967.

Ah, but they didn't win, so when it came out that their instrumental prowess was not all that their earnest TV performances made it out to be, there was no egg on anyone's face. Milli, though . . . Milli won. And somebody had to take the blame.

The Milli Vanilli story began in 1988 in Germany, where Farian — in time honored conveyor belt pop fashion — combined a team of killer studio vocalists, Brad Howe, Charles Shaw and John Davis, with a pair of great looking front men, German born Rob Pilatus and Frenchman Fabrice Morvan, christened them from the Turkish for "positive force," and unleashed them onto the Eurobeat dance floors.

It was a brilliant combination. Of course, it later became de rigeur to describe Pilatus and Morvan as talentless puppets, simply lip-synching the songs they had no part of. But as the hits piled up, it was Pilatus and Morvan who starred in the videos, dancing well, looking great, dreadlocks to die for . . . maybe they didn't sing on their records, but they did everything else involved with the promotion. In other words, Mr. Critic, they probably had a lot more talent than you. (And, they *could* sing — which would be where the problems started.)

Of course the critics hated Milli Vanilli — they hate most things that make no bones about their brainlessness, which go out simply to make you dance, make you buy, make you sing along in a very loud voice. But the industry adored them (probably for the same reasons.) Milli Vanilli's debut album, ALL OR NOTHING, conquered Europe. Their second, GIRL, YOU KNOW IT'S TRUE, conquered the world. Million selling singles flew off it like machine gun fire. The Canadian Juno Award for Best International Album flew into Milli Vanilli's trophy cabinet, and the American Music Awards named them Best New Artist. By the time of the Grammys, in February 1990, it was doubtful whether any power on earth could stop Milli Vanilli from running away with it.

And so it transpired, but pride came before a fall. As Frank Farian began pre-production on the next Milli Vanilli album, Pilatus and Morvan delivered an unexpected ultimatum. They wanted to sing on the record.

It wasn't that bizarre a request. Simply pulling three once pre-fab names out of mid-air, the Monkees had made a similar demand. So, during the British glam rock explosion of the early-mid 1970's, did the Sweet and Mud.

Farian, however, was not to be swayed — and neither were Milli Vanilli. With a self confident determination which deserved a Grammy in its own right, they fired Farian and prepared to record their next album alone. Farian responded by going public with his dirty little secret. Milli Vanilli were no better than two-thirds of the Partridge Family, one-fifth of the Rubettes, the bulk of the Love Affair and just about every great record ever made by Kansenatz Katz, Jonathan King, Tony Burrows, Jeff Barry. They were a made up pop group!

Maybe it was a slow news week, maybe it wasn't. Either way, Farian's revelations (revelations! How important this entire matter had suddenly become) became headline news across the US. "Phony Baloney" screamed the New York Post. "Silli Vanilli" bellowed the same city's Daily News. Other organs were equally engorged and, with the Grammy committee weighing into the fray ("we're appalled"), it was too, too easy to overlook the subtext that underpinned all the self-righteous howling.

It was bad enough that Milli were indeed Silli, but how much worse that they weren't even homegrown Sillis. In other words, how dare these dreadful Germans and French types pull so much wool over the eyes of upright American pop kids?

The fall-out was painfully predictable. Milli Vanilli were stripped of their Grammy and when, at a subsequent press conference, they performed *Girl You Know It's True* without a hint of backing tape shenanigans — they could have turned in the greatest virtuoso performance in the world, but the watching hacks were still going to shoot them down in flames. And they did.

Milli Vanilli ended there, crushed not by their own "lack" of "talent", nor even by the "fraud" which was the Grammy folks' excuse for stripping them of the award. They were crushed because they could be, because the media demanded it and because nobody — not the rock historians who claim to know everything about everything, but conveniently forgot about pop's proud precedents; nor the fans who hitherto hadn't cared a toss for who or what performed on the records; nor even the band's own record company, who'd apparently been in on the joke all along — had the balls to stand up and say, "it really doesn't matter."

Because it didn't — but, of course, it did. On April 2, 1998, Rob Pilatus, just 32 years old, died following an overdose of drugs and alcohol. It wasn't an accident.

Discography:
Singles
- *Girl You Know It's True / Magic Touch* (Arista 9781, 1989)
- *Baby Don't Forget My Number / Too Much Monkey Business* (Arista 9832, 1989)
- *Girl I'm Gonna Miss You / All Or Nothing* (Arista 9870, 1989)
- *Blame It On The Rain / Dance With A Devil* (Arista 9904, 1989)
- *All Or Nothing / Dreams To Remember* (Arista 9923, 1990)

Albums
- ALL OR NOTHING (Hansa 594580, 1988)
- ALL OR NOTHING — THE REMIX ALBUM (Hansa 599790, 1989)
- GIRL YOU KNOW IT'S TRUE (Arista 8592, 1989)
- QUICK MOVES — THE REMIX ALBUM (Arista 8622, 1990)
- THE MOMENT OF TRUTH (Arista [import], 1991)

~ 32 ~
Take That

1995: *Back For Good*

Take That was the most popular teen pop sensation in Britain since the 1960's, outselling every English group since the Beatles, dominating the UK charts throughout the first half of the 1990's, and unleashing two separate solo careers which seem set to continue that domination into the next century. Quite an achievement for a band that was conceived, in the first place, as a homegrown response to the New Kids On The Block.

The New Kids' British invasion was never as convincing as past American idols — a fate which was dictated, wryly enough, by precisely the same factors as made them such a smash in America. They were too "American."

In the past, Cassidy, Jackson, even the Osmond Brothers, had taken on an almost stateless appeal, musically, culturally and conversationally. They didn't ram their Americanness down their audience's throats, they didn't deck out in baseball caps and letterman jackets, they didn't look like they'd just spent their summer vacation hanging out on the street corner. Their accents simply conferred a touch of glamour, their upbringing a taste of paradise.

New Kids On The Block, on the other hand, arrived with both a music and a string of cultural reference points which translated only as long as the boys looked cute. The moment they tried to toughen up, adopt the street style smarts which they hoped would prolong their American life span, their British audience turned away. Which was precisely what Take That must have been hoping would happen.

Their early repertoire, too, dipped its feet into new jack R&B territory, tinged with mainstream balladry. But very early on, the realization dawned that adult contemporary themes work just as well within a market which essentially wanted only love and affection from its idols. Seemingly overnight, and certainly before there was an established band "sound," Take That redesigned their repertoire, and broadened their horizons immeasurably.

The group was founded by Gary Barlow, a prodigious teen musician long before Take That came into being. At 14, he was organist in comedian Ken Dodd's supporting band, and during the mid-1980's, one of his earliest songs, *Let's Pray for Christmas*, came close to winning a song writing contest staged by the BBC afternoon television show, Pebble Mill At One. It was Barlow's meeting with former soccer apprentice Mark Owen and soap actor Robbie Williams, however, which truly sparked his ambition, and in 1987, the trio formed a band together, Cutest Rush.

Cutest Rush never recorded, but coming into the orbit of producer / manager Nigel Martin Smith, they were invited to become part of a larger combo, cut in the vein of New Kids on the Block. They agreed and, joined by Jason Orange and Howard Donald — former members of the Street Beat breakdancing troupe — they became Take That in 1990.

Smith originally placed the quintet on the nightclub circuit, before releasing their debut single, *Do What U Like*, on his own independent Dance UK label in July, 1991. It was a competent single, but far more important was the accompanying video, with its lingering glimpses of the boys . . . and their bare bottoms. A minor controversy erupted with predictable speed, and by the fall, Take That had signed with RCA, and rounded out 1991 with their first hit, a No. 38 placing for *Promises*.

Two further 45's followed, with the third, *Once You've Tasted Love*, making No. 47 before a cover of Tavares' *It Only Takes A Minute* (also covered by Jonathan King) gave Take That their first British Top 10 hit, in June, 1992. TAKE THAT AND PARTY, their first album, followed, debuting at No. 5, then climbing to No. 2 as a new single, *A Million Love Songs*, reached the Top 10. At the end of the year, the group took home seven awards at the Smash Hits Awards, and six months later, a BRIT award winning cover of Barry Manilow's *Could It Be Magic* pushed them into the Top 3 for the first time. *Why Can't I Wake Up With You*, in February, 1993, made it to No. 2, and from there on in, it was No. 1's all the way. Between July, 1993, and June, 1996, all but one of Take That's next nine singles hit the top spot in Britain — the exception, *Love Ain't Here Any More*, reached No. 3. The group's second album, EVERYTHING CHANGES, and their third, NOBODY ELSE, continued the tradition.

It was a phenomenal perfor-mance all round, all the more so since the band's most immediate selling point, their youth and correspondingly youthful good looks, accounted for only a part of their actual appeal. Following on from that off-color debut, strong sexual (and homosexual) undercurrents in their videos saw Take That's audience spread through both the gay and kitsch loving communities, with the bondage and battery laden *How Deep Is Your Love* (the Bee Gees hit, executed with razor sharp precision and aplomb) taking such fantasies to the wildest extremes imaginable —

it begins with a kidnap, it ends with a massacre, and there really aren't too many teen dream pop videos which end by killing off their main characters.

Although their biggest hits tended to be covers, Gary Barlow himself was a singer songwriter whose own talent was the rival of many of the songwriters Take That covered. And while the upsurge of the Oasis / Suede / Blur-led Britpop scene in the mid-1990's did dent Take That's popularity among some of their younger pop constituents, it actually reinforced their appeal to others, particularly after they turned in a chart-topping duet with 60's idol Lulu, on 1993's *Relight My Fire*. Not only did the song introduce Take That to a vast, and hitherto untapped, audience of older listeners, it also shaped much of the group's subsequent output, as they strived to become the first British pop group since the Beatles who could truly claim to appeal to every generation that encountered them.

Yet there was trouble in paradise. Robbie Williams had long been developing a tabloid reputation for a certain "wildness", while rumors that he was dissatisfied with the way Take That was developing were rife even before the group's third album was released. His comparative silence throughout that set only compounded the whispering, particularly when he broke that silence by announcing his plans to launch a solo career. He finally quit Take That in July, 1995 — and was promptly deleted from the band's very history.

With Orwellian ruthlessness, Williams' name and image were pulled from every piece of promotional and commercial material Take That could lay their hands on — they even removed his face from the cover of the American release of NOBODY ELSE — and when Williams' first solo single, a cover of George Michael's *Freedom*, appeared to little applause, it seemed likely that he would never be heard of again. Within two years, however, he had turned even the critical mockery around, scored a No. 1 hit with the amazing *Millennium*, and was watching his second solo album go places where Take That had never even dreamed of — including a lot of "serious" music fans' collections. *Angels*, his first hit, was the greatest record Elton John was now way too old to make, while the James Bondaged *Millennium* and the daftly self analytical *Strong* both proved that even icons have to laugh occasionally. The title of his US debut album, *The Ego has Landed*, proved they can also do it out loud.

Williams' defection did not end Take That's internal difficulties. Though he continued to put a brave face on things, Barlow, too, was losing interest and faith — particularly when continued attempts to break Take That in America foundered upon any number of indifferent walls. It was hideously ironic, then, that just as the Stateside worm was finally beginning to turn, and *Back For Good* was beginning to nibble at the American Top 40, Take That split up, on February 13, 1996.

The group bade farewell with the *How Deep Is Your Love* single, and a greatest hits package which simply overwhelms the listener with its magnitude. Barlow, however, had no time for farewells, commencing work immediately upon his first album, a task which also occupied Mark Owen. Both, like Williams, enjoid some success. Both may, as Williams is certain to do, use their time with Take That as the springboard to far greater musical achievements. But even if they don't, still they've already made their mark on musical history as members of what was one of the most personally fascinating, and commercially stunning British teen-pop phenomenons, not only of the 90's, but of the Rock and Roll era as a whole.

Discography:
Singles
  ○ *Back For Good / Love Ain't Here Anymore* (Arista 12848, 1284)
Albums
  ○ TAKE THAT AND PARTY (RCA 66221, 1992)
  ○ EVERYTHING CHANGES (RCA [import], 1993)
  ○ NOBODY ELSE (RCA 73421279092, 1995)
  ○ TAKE THAT (Arista 8800, 1995)

~ 33 ~
The Spice Girls

1996: *Wannabe*

A Martian, or at least, an alternative rock minded American, arriving in Britain in mid-1996 and switching on Top Of The Pops that first Friday, would probably have wondered what had happened.

Against the traditional backdrop of seething teen enthusiasm, an act was introduced which, the show's hostess insisted, was bringing some Riot Grrl action to the chart. But would that be Riot Grrl, as in the upsurge in staunchly feminist rockers which had emerged onto the post-Lollapalooza scene in the shape of Babes In Toyland, L7 and Hole? Or Riot Grrl, as in the misappropriation of an already over-used cliché, for the benefit of a new pop phenomenon whose feminism was, in any case, no more or less a marketing gimmick than Mike Nesmith's hat, Ringo Starr's nose, or Jimmy Osmond's Little? The Spice Girls had arrived, and with them all bets for the remainder of the decade were off.

At its basest level, the Spice Girls' entire existence was derived from just two role models — musically, Take That, and culturally, Madonna. But whereas the former Ms Ciccione had fought to become all things to all listeners, the Spice Girls divided the work between them.

There was the sexy Ginger Spice (Geri Halliwell); the scary Scary Spice (Melanie Brown); the posh Posh Spice (Victoria Addams); the sporty Sporty Spice (Melanie Chisholm); and the blonde inflatable Baby Spice (Emma Bunton), five very separate, extraordinarily colorful, persona with which a fiendishly well-oiled publicity machine would begin inculcating the public almost before the group's first record was even recorded.

Carefully salted press coverage suggested the five identities and a brilliantly designed video cemented them. And with the Girls themselves riding a wave of interest rooted half in their overall vibe of all-girl good time feminism, and half in the mood enhancing Cool Britannia which was dragging the country out of the mire of the past decade of social under-achievement, by the time *Wannabe* hit the airwaves, there was no hotter tip for the top of the chart. The Spice Girls had made it, and all their detractors could do was try and figure what they made it from.

The individual Spice Girls were recruited, in true Monkees-manufactory style, by a summer, 1993, advertisement calling for five "lively" girls to join a musical group. All five arrived with at least a modicum of theatrical, modeling and, in Sexy's case, nude experience behind them. They also, however, developed a personal bond which allowed them to dump their original svengali within two months of starting out, and spend the next two years struggling to establish their own vision of the group.

Several record companies and management teams tried to take them on, but with remarkable foresight, the Spice Girls alone truly understand their own game plan — that there should be no readily defined "leader" of the group, and that all five should spend equal time in the spotlight, both on and offstage.

This was not, of course, an original concept — the Beatles and (again) the Monkees had made a similar connection, while the Osmonds and the Jacksons, once past the precocious charms of their junior members, were also regarded as equals by their fan clubs. Recent years — indeed, recent decades — however, had seen such egalitarianism abandoned, as the teen dream dynasty of New Edition, New Kids On The Block, even Take That, built their own charms around one easily isolated front man. Not for the last time, the Spice Girls were out on a limb which so few people comprehended that, even after they finally signed to Virgin Records, they remained managerless. But finally, late 1995 saw Annie Lennox manager Simon Fuller come on board, and work could now begin.

All five Spice Girls were now living in a house together, reinforcing the sisters-together image which their fierce independence had already set in motion. Now, with Fuller and songwriter Elliot Kennedy behind them, and *Wannabe*, the Spice Girls' first single, on the horizon, the pre-release promotion could begin.

Wannabe slammed into the UK chart at No. 1, the first debut single by an all-female band ever to enter the charts at the top — let alone stay there for seven weeks. By the end of the year, *Wannabe* had reached number one in 21 other countries, even as their second single, *Say You'll Be There*, followed up with sales of 200,000 copies a week. SPICE, the Girls' debut album, was released at the end of the year, accompanied by their first ballad, and third successive British No. 1, *2 Become 1*.

The Spice Girls' appeal was peculiarly egalitarian. Girls liked them because they wanted to be them; boys liked them because . . . well because. And the marketing behind the group was no less even handed. Spice clothes, Spice dolls, Spice soda — the girls signed endorsements, it seemed, like other stars signed autographs, until it was impossible to turn around that Christmas without encountering another grinning Spice bawble, clutched in the paw of another Spice clone. Madonna, it was once said, took boudoir chic out of the bedroom and into the High Street stores. The Spice Girls were the shoppers who bought it — and then sold it on again. And they had only just begun.

Having sewn up the rest of the world in less than six months, the Spice Girls' assault on the United States commenced in January, 1997, with the consecutive releases of *Wannabe* and SPICE. Again, the results were spectacular, and duplicating their European schedule, both *Say You'll Be There* and *2 Become 1* followed, leading up to the release of SPICE WORLD, the Girls' second LP, and a feature film of the same name.

It was also, however, the start of a backlash which saw the media (particularly in the UK) pick up on every last flaw in the Spice Girls' campaign, then magnify it beyond all proportion. "Fundamentally, we are all alike," Geri Spice told Britain's Hello magazine that November. "Think of Prince Charles, a homeless person, yourself, Mahatma Gandhi, and they all want one thing. To be healthy and have fun." But "fun" certainly seemed to be in short supply. Booed offstage in Spain, where they were finally laying to rest the media insistence that they could not perform live (by proving that they could — even if they weren't very good at it); faced with plummeting record sales; and saddled with a critically hammered debut movie; the Spice Girls suddenly found themselves a hot property among British bookmakers alone. The wager was, "how soon would they break up?"

The Spice Girls' commercial bubble remained far from bursting, however. Widely trumpeted "lower than expected" sales of their second album, SPICE WORLD were nevertheless high enough to see it debut at No. 1 in Britain, and No. 8 in the US, while their year-old first album continued to sell in excess of 60,000 copies a week. Two singles culled from SPICE WORLD, *Spice Up Your Life* and *Too Much*, both made similar chart-topping appearances in Britain, establishing the Spice Girls as the first group in history to hit No. 1 with each of its first six singles.

Meanwhile, the Girls' SPICE WORLD movie was Britain's box office smash of the Christmas period, raking in $3.8 million within just four days of its December 26 release, and this in spite of the movie itself suffering a severe case of the wobblies before it was even out of the cutting room.

The deaths, in swift succession, of Gianni Versace, Princess Diana and Mother Theresa all forced hasty edits in dialogue: the Girls' avowed intent of marketing a true family movie apparently precluding any mention of the newly deceased. Boxer Frank Bruno, one of the movies' guest stars, withdrew early on in the production, with an unnamed associate subsequently describing the Girls as "unpleasant"; but most alarming of all was the November 19 arrest, on child pornography charges, of glam superhero Gary Glitter, who was to appear in the film performing his 1973 hit *Leader Of The Gang* with the Spices. According to the British press, attempts to excise Glitter's appearance were met with a $16 million demand for compensation by the singer.

A spokesperson for the Spice Girls' label, Virgin, too, remained unimpressed by reports of the quintet's imminent demise. "People have been knocking the Spice Girls since the beginning," she snapped, "and they still went on to become the biggest band in the world."

Yet the doomsayers did get something right — all was not well in Spiceworld. Manager Simon Fuller was despatched in late 1997. Ginger Geri Spice followed in May, 1998, armed with the $8 million personal fortune which recent industry experts had suggested each member of the group was privy to, and already threatening the solo career which would eventually burst into view a year later.

At first, her departure was kept deathly quiet — indeed, the Spice Girls played their first show as a four piece (Geri would not, could not, be replaced) before anybody even realized Ginger had quit. And such was the hysteria surrounding the group that a crowd of several thousand Norwegian fans didn't seem at all phased by the group's explanation that she was simply ill. And having proven that they could carry on without The Artist Formerly Known As Ginger, they proceeded to do so, completing a sell-out American tour; and scoring yet another pair of British No. 1's, the summer smash *Viva Forever* and the now inevitable Christmas chart topper *Goodbye*.

The Spice Girls' ability to survive what would, for any other band in their position, have been a very painful amputation, was remarkable. But it was their fans' willingness to stick with the group through those tumultuous events which indicated the true depth of feeling which the Spice Girls had tapped into. No simple pop phenomenon, the Spice Girls transcended mere musical fashion, to become true media personalities — possibly pop's first, and certainly the most successful, since the heyday of the 80's glitterati, Simon Le Bon, Madonna, Bob Geldof and Co.

When Posh Spice became a Spice Mother, she and her soccer playing husband David Beckham were swamped by well wishers. Dozens of fans turned up at the hospital with gifts. Geri Halliwell sent flowers. Scary's newborn daughter, too, arrived into a world which feted her almost as much as it did her mother. Quite simply, the Spice Girls could do no wrong, and even when they did, it didn't matter.

For as long as the Spice Girls have been on the scene, the only thing more inevitable than their success has been their downfall. But at the time of writing, three years on from *Wannabe*, that moment seems as far away as ever.

Discography:
Singles
  ○ *Wannabe / Bumper To Bumper* (Virgin 38579, 1996)
  ○ *Say You'll Be There / Take Me Home* (Virgin 38592, 1996)

- ○ *2 Become 1 / One Of These Girls* (Virgin 38604, 1996)
- ○ *Spice Up Your Life /* (Virgin 38620, 1997)
- ○ *Too Much /* (Virgin 38630, 1997)
- ○ *Stop / Something Kinda Funny* (Virgin 38641, 1998)
- ○ *Goodbye /* (Virgin 38652, 1998)

Albums
- ○ SPICE (Virgin 42174, 1996)
- ○ SPICEWORLD (Virgin 45111, 1997)

~ 34 ~
Babylon Zoo

1996: *Spaceman*

"Don't look now, but there's an alien coming." Babylon Zoo's *Spaceman* to be precise, a chart-topper in 18 countries worldwide in 1996, and it wasn't hard to spot its appeal. Mr. Babylon Zoo himself, Jas Mann, was obscenely photogenic, *Spaceman* was irresistibly catchy, and if anyone needed further convincing, it had a killer video which combined the two. Plus, Mann himself was from another planet, which meant he'd already got the X-Files market sewn up, before he even opened his mouth. The rest of our planet simply followed meekly in their wake, and that despite the knowledge that Earth, a passing interest in David Bowie aside, hadn't made stars out of too many spacemen.

But that's because he turned out not to be a spaceman after all. Rather, "people picked up on the first thing I created, which was this spaceman character, but rather than little green men from space, it was using the image like a writer would create a character in a film. The spaceman is someone who doesn't like the space, the environment that he's in, the prototype societies of this world, the geometric forms of boxes we live in, the space, man, and wants to go somewhere else, another planet, find another way of life."

Echoing, indeed, the David Bowie of long before, Mann continued, "I've always been interested in science fiction, I've always been interested in what's beyond the normality of life, and combining it with music." And that's all sorts of music, too. Jeff Barry, the orchestral brain behind countless Bond movies, was considering working with Mann, as Mann himself went into the studio with New York production superman Arthur Baker.

Mann enjoyed the conflict. "I like rock music, and even though Babylon Zoo isn't traditional rock, it isn't retro rock. It's music that uses a lot of organic elements as well as the futuristic elements." To that end, the New York Times described the Zoo's BOY WITH THE X RAY EYES album as post-grunge, which of course it wasn't, but it did at least place the band, and the monster pop smash they rode in on, in a totally different light to most of their homeland's mid-1990's exports. Indeed, throughout *Spaceman*'s life span, Babylon Zoo's greatest asset was that they had absolutely nothing to do with anything

Britain had produced in years. As Mann explained, "we came along and we released this record, and visually we did what we did, and what had gone on before us, literally months before, was so different to what we were doing that within the media, it was a severely hard pill to swallow. But with the people who buy the records it wasn't."

It didn't help either that Babylon Zoo's "big break" came when *Spaceman* was picked up for a Levi ad. It promptly became the fastest selling debut single in British chart history, 250,000 copies in a week, bigger than Band Aid, bigger than the Beatles, bigger, even, than Stiltskin, the last band to land the magic Levis touch — and who were never heard of again, ha,ha.

Babylon Zoo, as it transpired, suffered the same sorry fate. 1999 brought the group's second album — a remarkably good second album, packing an excellent remake of Mott The Hoople's *Honaloochie Boogie*, among other things — and it flopped. But at the time of *Spaceman*, Mann was convincingly confident Babylon Zoo wouldn't go the same way, a conclusion he arrived at once *Spaceman* had topped the chart in five countries. The commercial was only shown in four.

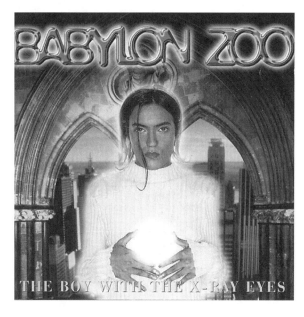

"People are always a bit dubious, a group that suddenly comes along and breaks all the records with their first single, it's one of those things. But I don't want to start competing with myself at this stage, I've always done the same thing, from day one when I recorded the album — or most of it — in my bedroom, till the day I released it, just take every day as it goes and get on with the next thing that's ahead and never think about it. I think it's become a mass bubblegum society where the flavors are gone really quick, so you just move onto your next record.

"We've been described as everything, and we don't really fit into many molds, but I suppose you have to in certain places. All the music that was around when I was growing up, your next door neighbor's into Black Sabbath and Led Zeppelin or whatever, even though I never really was, I was aware of it, and whatever we fit into, those influences will impact."

Discography:
Singles
　○ *Spaceman* / (mixes) (Capitol 58558, 1996)
Albums
　○ BOY WITH THE X-RAY EYES (Capitol 37204, 1996)
　○ KING KONG GROOVER (Capitol [import], 1999)

~ 35 ~
Gala

1996: *Freed From Desire*

The face of Europop as it embraces the new millennium, Milan-born Gala left the old century behind with one of the crucial dance hits of the decade, the exuberant *Freed From Desire*, a magnificent slice of insidiously insistent pop whose easily misheard lyrics ("my boyfriend's got no money, he's got his trumblies") only amplified its other attributes. Arriving in Britain and America out of nowhere, it seemed, but dominating the club scene for the remainder of the decade, *Freed From Desire* became one of those songs from which there can never be any escape. Hear it once and you're hooked — whether you want to be or not.

Gala took her name from Salvador Dali's wife, and from the Russian dancer Gala Ulanova. Escaping a strict schooling in her native Italy, she traveled extensively, studying whatever took her fancy — flamenco at Madrid's renowned Amor De Dios dance school; African dance under the guidance of Babekar M'Baye from the National Ballet of Senegal; and photography at the Superstudio and the Laban Center in London — before moving to New York to attend the Tisch School of Arts, within the New York University.

Never did she consider music, however, preferring to work on the other side of the lens, as a video director. And it was in Italy, while "taking pictures of a deejay," that this deejay himself discovered her, in 1995. Her debut recording, the sultry disco burner *XS* was included on the ORIGINALE RADICALE MUSICALE compilation, and emboldened by the response to the track, Gala cut her debut single, *Everyone Has Inside*, for fall, 1995, release. It promptly went to No. 1 on the Italian chart.

Produced by the award winning team of Molella and Phil Jay, *Freed From Desire* was an effortless follow-up, topping her homeland's chart for a month, before exploding out across the rest of Europe — Spain, France, Belgium, the Netherlands, Germany, Scandinavia and Greece, and finally cracking the U.K in late 1996. *Freed From Desire* sold half a million in Britain, and while its American success was less pronounced, still the record achieved major club radio airplay. Gala's third single, *Let A Boy Cry*, appeared in Europe in January, 1997, another pop-dance classic which earned — among a myriad other honors — a platinum record in Belgium. An album, COME INTO MY LIFE (accompanied by a single version of the epic title track) followed that November.

Like so many before her, Gala's actual musical achievements ensure that the pop crown rests very uneasily on her head — an unease, of course, which only cements it further into place. In many respects, the best pop acts — a hotly debatable coterie which includes the likes of ABBA, the Carpenters, the Jackson Five and All Saints — are those to whom the honor devolves naturally; those whose success (or more accurately, whose appeal) is developed naturally, and are not the product of a top level brainstorm meeting in the accountancy department.

Gala, a multi-talent whom some Italian critics have already compared to Prince, readily takes her place in that company, writing and performing with an intensity which owes little to any preconceived notions of her audience, and everything to a need, simply, to succeed in whatever she tries. *Freed From Desire* achieved that with room to spare. Her debut album proved that it wasn't a fluke.

Discography:
Singles
  ○ *Freed From Desire* / (mixes) (ZYX 8479-8, 1996)
Albums
  ○ COME INTO MY LIFE (Big Life[import], 1996)

~ 36 ~
Hanson

1997: MMM Bop

Though it would be five years more before Hanson burst onto the domestic scene with the insanely contagious *MMM Bop*, the brothers Isaac, Taylor and Zac had been rehearsing and recording in their Tulsa, Oklahoma garage since 1992.

All were pre-teens at the time, something that swiftly encouraged comparisons with the Jackson Five, the Osmonds and the DeFrancos once the band did emerge. Their tastes, however, were precocious — even around the family dinner table, their repertoire was based in 50's and 60's rock and soul standards, picked up from the TIME LIFE HISTORY OF ROCK type albums which their father collected when work took him and his family to South America in the early 1990's.

The band's first stab at getting a record deal came when they approached music business lawyer Christopher Sabec and performed á cappella for him. Sabec was suitably impressed and became Hanson's manager. However, attempts to take them further were dashed when five separate record labels passed on the brothers' talents. Hanson contended themselves with a pair of self-released singles and an album, BOOMERANG.

It was with their second indie album, MMM BOP, in 1995, that the group's fortunes — and outlook — began to change. Playing their own instruments with at least above average competence and absorbing a contemporary dance / hip hop groove, Hanson was signed to Mercury and paired with producer Steve Lironi.

Over the next year, the group pieced together what became IN THE MIDDLE OF NOWHERE with further collaborators Barry Mann & Cynthia Weil, Desmond Child, the Dust Brothers and Mark Hudson — of the 13 tracks on the album, no less than nine were dignified with outside assistance ... although the band's growing coterie of admirers were swift to point out that four of them weren't.

Featuring re-recordings of *MMM Bop*, *Thinking Of You* and *With You In Your Dreams* from the garage days, the album was released in spring 1997 with a Tamara Davis directed video for *MMM Bop* previewing the brothers shortly before. A major press and media campaign was launched, raising Hanson's overall profile far beyond that normally associated with teenage / boy groups — the "serious" press was courted as diligently as the teen sheets, with the sheer adventurousness of the record being as key a selling point as the brothers' resemblance to past teen idols. The hard work paid off when *MMM Bop* crashed into the US chart at No. 13 in April. The album followed it skywards and, overnight, Hanson was established as the teen sensation of 1997.

They were not, of course, above the standard machinations of their market — the Christmas albums which were mandatory among the young bucks of the 1970's (and revived by New Kids On The Block) were still a power in the marketplace and Hanson's SNOWED IN, released in late fall, disappointed nobody.

At the same time, however, serious attempts underway to portray Hanson as something more than a bunch of puppet popsters remained. Their courageous garageland beginnings were resuscitated as THREE CAR GARAGE, taking the edge off a (again apposite) collectors market, while the standard accusations that the band couldn't play their own instruments particularly well were dismissed with the release of LIVE FROM ALBERTANE (a line from the lyric to *Man From Milwaukee*), recorded in Seattle during Hanson's first stadium tour.

With highlights ranging from the audience's non-stop barrage of high pitched keening, to a genuine drum solo from Zac, LIVE AT ALBERTANE ranks alongside any 70's-era teen live album (the Osmonds and Cassidy included) not only as in terms of sheer excitement and exuberance, but also in relation to what it tells us about the band's own aspirations.

Sensibly, Hanson didn't race to follow up IN THE MIDDLE OF NOWHERE, preferring to leave the field open to the wealth of imitators and would-be rivals who flooded through in their wake. Britney Spears and Cristina Aguilera started here. So did the wide screen breakouts of the Backstreet Boys and N Sync. After years in the US pop wilderness, suddenly teen dollars were as powerful as they had ever been in the past — and as dictatorial as well. No matter that the majority of acts thrown to the lions following Hanson's breakthrough were, unlike Hanson, considerably less autonomous or musically ambitious, still daytime pop TV became home to more acres of fresh teenage flesh than an Eagle Scouts jamboree.

Hanson finally returned to action in spring 2000. THIS TIME AROUND was a logical progression from its predecessor, both musically and in maturity — again, an insistence that Hanson were not to be simply filed away with the jail bait, to be torn off the bedroom wall the moment somebody cuter came along. Guest spots from Jonny Lang and Blues Traveler's John Popper made a serious bid for musical credibility, while the Hanson / Hanson / Hanson song writing credits indicated just how far the band had grown since their debut.

Discography:
Singles
  o *MMM Bop* / (mixes) (Mercury 574261, 1997)
  o *I Will Come To You* / (mixes) (Mercury 568132, 1997)
  o *Weird* / *Speechless* (Mercury 568541, 1998)
  o *This Time Around* / (mixes) (Island 562716, 2000)
  o *If Only* / (mixes) (Island 562750, 2000)
Albums
  o MIDDLE OF NOWHERE (Mercury 534615, 1997)
  o SNOWED IN (Mercury 536717, 1997)
  o LIVE FROM ALBERTANE (Mercury 538240, 1998)
  o THREE CAR GARAGE: THE INDIE RECORDINGS (Mercury 558399, 1998)
  o THIS TIME AROUND (Island 155055, 2000)

~ 37 ~
All Saints

1998: *Never Ever*

Of course the Spice Girls were not going to have the field to themselves for long, although when a truly viable competitor did emerge, it was from a musical base which few observers would have predicted. A host of purported successors had already come and gone — Vanilla, Eternal, Cleopatra, N-Tyce — but it was west London's All Saints (named for the Ladbroke Grove street which housed their first demo studio) who finally besieged the citadel, and All Saints who broke down the walls. But though they were visually cut from precisely the same cloth as the Spicers — two brunettes, one blonde, and one West Indian descendent — that was where the comparisons ended.

All Saints formed in 1993, when Melanie Blatt and Shaznay Lewis began working at the All Saints Road studio. There they met up with R&B vocalist Simone Rainford, and in early 1995, ZTT released the group's first single, a cover of Atlantic Starr's *Silver Shadow*. It flopped, but the trio did get out on that fall's Smash Hits road show tour, and overcoming Rainford's departure, Blatt and Lewis cut a follow-up single, *Let's Get Started*. It was not a very appropriate choice — by January, 1996, All Saints were all but finished, after ZTT dropped them.

Hooking up with Canadian Nicole Appleton and later, her elder sister Nathalie, All Saints were relaunched as a quartet in late 1996, and went back to the studio with Karl Gordon, a one time member of the British rap legend Outlaw Posse. The ensuing demo, *I Know Where It's At*, was enough to interest first, manager John Benson, then London Records, and finally, producer Nellee Hooper. Nine months later, a storming new interpretation of the same song, built around a piano refrain borrowed from Steely Dan's *The Fez*, soared to No. 4 in the UK, and gave the group a sizable hit elsewhere around Europe and Asia.

The group's appeal was immediate and obvious. Retaining much of the big sister appeal of the Spice Girls, All Saints nevertheless eschewed both the cartoon characterization of their predecessors, and their blatant sexual coprophilia, replacing it with a solid, but never workmanlike, soulfulness which defied their apparent intentions. Indeed, media attempts to portray All Saints as any kind of answer to the Spice Girls were furiously denied, not so much verbally, however, as with the sheer strength of the quartet's music.

All Saints' first British No. 1 followed with the release, in November, 1997, of *Never Ever*. Topping the chart early in 1998, and with their self-titled debut album arriving to similar success and plaudits, All Saints were one of the sensations of the 1997 BRIT awards ... then caused an even greater stir when they announced their next single: a cover of the Red Hot Chili Peppers' *Under The Bridge*, backed by an equally audacious take on Labelle's *Lady Marmalade*.

Blithely, however, it swept to the top (*Under The Bridge* peaked at No. 4 in Britain.) *Bootie Call*, in September, 1998, brought them another chart topper, and just to round out a sensational year, All Saints' American breakthrough came with *I Know Where It's At.* And so, despite continuous media reports of inter-band rivalry, splits and disaster, All Saints approach the 21st century from a position of considerable pop authority.

Discography:
Singles
- *I Know Where It's At* / (mix) (Polygram 570112, 1997)
- *Never Ever* / *I Remember* (Polygram 570179, 1998)
- *Under The Bridge* / *Lady Marmalade* (Polygram, 1998)
- *Bootie Call* / *Get Down* (Polygram, 1998)
- *War Of Nerves* / *Inside* (Polygram 570361, 1999)

Albums
- ALL SAINTS (London 828997, 1998)
- REMIX ALBUM (London 556063, 1998)

~ 38 ~
The Backstreet Boys

1998: *As Long As You Love Me*

Take That's reign was just coming to its close when Backstreet Boys emerged, a fortuitous coincidence to say the least, even if the Americans' musical direction was wholly removed from the Mancunians' majestic balladry. Dance and R&B oriented, with a new jack edge which cast them in a wholly different light to almost anything targeted at the teen pop market in the past (NKOTB included), the middle class white Backstreet Boys skewed so many established American industry formulae that for two years, they could barely even get arrested in their homeland — at the same time as the rest of world was going crazy for them.

The Backstreet Boys formed around Lexington Kentucky cousins Kevin Richardson and Brian Littrell, singers since childhood, and seasoned veterans of everything from church choirs to local festivals, where they performed updated doo-wop and Boyz II Men-ish R&B. The pair remained together until Richardson upped and moved to Orlando, Florida, where he landed a gig as a tour guide at Disneyland.

Meantime, Orlando natives Howie Dorough and A. J. McLean, plus native New Yorker Nick Carter, came together on the local acting circuit, continually running in to one another at auditions for local commercials, TV and theater gigs. Discovering that their musical tastes dovetailed in the direction of harmonic soul — discovering, too, that they could execute the music with effortless ease — they formed a trio of their own and moved onto the Orlando club circuit.

A friend introduced them to Kevin Richardson. He called Littrell down to join him, and by mid-1994, the Backstreet Boys — named after a local flea market — were working with producer friend Louis J Pearlman, and recruited the Donna and Johnny Wright management team. A deal with Jive / Zomba followed, and by the end of the year, producers Veit Renn and Tim Allen had the Backstreet Boys in the studio, piecing together what became their eponymous debut album.

BACKSTREET BOYS was released throughout Europe and North America in late 1995 and became an immediate smash. Canada fell for it big time, most of continental Europe sent it rocketing into the local Top 10, and in Britain, the Backstreet Boys were named Best Newcomers of 1995 at the prestigious Smash Hits Awards. At home, however, even their biggest hit, the smooth, cool *We've Got It Goin' On*, couldn't scrape higher than the bottom end of the chart, and it would be two years more before the group's status finally started to rise.

Hard work and hot promotion pushed the Backstreet Boys' Stateside star, but it was 1997's European BACKSTREET'S BACK album which marked the turning point. A US version, bringing together cuts from both this latest opus and its predecessor was released under the title BACKSTREET BOYS, and, backed by the singles *Quit Playin' Games (With My Heart)* (from the first album) and *As Long as You Love Me* (from the second), it finally gatecrashed the US chart. And how. 27 million copies sold, a total of five massive hit singles, a profile in Rolling Stone — suddenly, nobody could ignore them.

"The best thing is that we've achieved incredible success in the US," Kevin told Smash Hits. "I think it's exceeded all of our expectations. We're going to be getting a diamond award which is a new award that Billboard have created for artists that have sold over ten times platinum — that's over ten million albums. That's a pretty incredible achievement."

The band's sudden elevation wasn't without its sobering side — a well-publicized break with their original management team and, more seriously, Brian's heart surgery. Balanced against both, however, were complete recoveries from both setbacks, and the release of MILLENNIUM, the Backstreet Boys' third album and an immediate record breaker — first week sales not only knocked would-be pop icon Ricky Martin off the US No. 1 slot, they also shattered all existing records with a mountain moving 1.13 million copies sold. And, whatever else might befall the band, that's an achievement which will be hard to take away from them.

The Backstreet Boys

Discography:
Singles
- *We Got It Going On* / (remix) (Jive 42329, 1995)
- *Quit Playing Games* / (remix) (Jive 42472, 1997)
- *As Long As You Love Me* / *Everytime I Close My Eyes* (Jive 434, 1997)
- *Everybody* / (remix) (Jive 42510, 1998)
- *All I Have To Give* / (remix) (Jive 42563, 1999)
- *I Want It That way* / *My Heart Stays With You* (BMG 52339, 1999)
- *We Got It Going On* / *Get Down* (BMG 51557, 1999)
- *Show Me The Meaning Of Being Lovely* / (BMG 25008, 2000)

Albums
- BACKSTREET BOYS / BACKSTREET'S BACK (Jive 41589, 1997)
- MILLENNIUM (Jive 41672, 1999)
- CHRISTMAS ALBUM (Jive 41681, 1999)

~ 39 ~
'N Sync

1998: *You Drive Me Crazy*

Orlando was hot, the new teen nerve center of America and, if the Backstreet Boys weren't proof enough of that, then the teenage vocal group 'N Sync surely was. The group formed in 1996 around two former members of the Disney Channel's Mickey Mouse Club (Britney Spears was part of the same troupe), singers J. C. Chasez and Justin Timberlake. Relocating to Nashville, the pair found themselves working on solo projects with the same vocal coach and songwriters, and when Timberlake returned to Orlando, where he hooked up with Chris Kirkpatrick, James Lance Bass and Joey Fatone, Chasez swiftly followed. The group's chosen name, of course, applied to their music and dance steps — they really were in sync. But it also turned out to be an acronym of either their names, or their nicknames: JustiN, ChriS, JoeY, LansteN (Bass) and JC.

Rehearsing in a remodeled local warehouse, the first song they ever sang together was the American national anthem. Their choice of Backroom Boys, however, was more indicative of the group's ambition, as they took on manager Johnny Wright, of New Kids On The Block fame, and Denniz Pop, renowned for his production work with Ace Of Base.

'N Sync's early successes — like the Backstreet Boys before them — came in Europe, where their self-titled debut album was originally released by the German label BMG Ariola Munich, while the thumping *I Want You Back* and *Tearing Up My Heart* both became continent-wide hits. 'N SYNC was finally released in the US in the spring of 1998 with the group supporting it by embarking first on a tour of the nation's roller rinks, then opening for Janet Jackson. The result was predictable — 'N SYNC went on to become one of the fastest selling debut albums of the year, hitting platinum status in America in August, just as the band gave its first televised concert . . . on the Disney Channel. The Backstreet Boys had originally been offered the gig, incidentally. They turned it down.

By the end of the year, *I Want You Back* had swept away with two honors at the Billboard Music Awards (Best Dance Clip and Best New Dance Act), and the band's second album, the seasonal HOME FOR CHRISTMAS, was preparing to become one of the fastest selling festive records of the decade.

Naturally the knockers were swift to descend, prophesying a swift end not only to 'N Sync, but to the boy band phenomenon in general. It wasn't to be — the success of the Backstreet Boys' MILLENNIUM in 1999 shocked observers; that of 'N Sync's second album, NO STRINGS ATTACHED, stunned them. Released March 21, 2000, first day sales amounted to 930,000 copies. Within a week, US sales alone approached 2.5 million, doubling the Backstreet Boys' first week sales record — a warming rejoinder to the increasingly bitter rivalry which existed between the two bands.

That rivalry warmed up even more when 'N Sync emerged from an ugly dispute with their management and jumped record labels — to the Backstreet Boys' own home at Jive. The title of the album, of course, referred to their new found freedom. The lead single, *Bye Bye Bye*, might well have been a further reminder of all that they'd left behind them as they pursued a new future of self-determination.

Discography:
Singles
- ○ *I Want You Back / Giddy Up* (RCA / BMG 65348, 1998)
- ○ *U Drive Me Crazy /* (remixes) (RCA / BMG 58815, 1998)
- ○ *God Must Have Spent A Little More Time /* (RCA / BMG 65685, 1999)
- ○ *For The Girl Who Has Everything /* (RCA / BMG 50792, 1999)
- ○ *Together Again /* (RCA / BMG 52017, 1999)
- ○ *Thinking Of You /* (RCA / BMG 63855, 1999)
- ○ *Bye Bye Bye /* (remix) (RCA / BMG 42681, 2000)
- ○ *I'll Never Stop /* (RCA / BMG 25071, 2000)
Albums
- ○ N SYNC (RCA / BMG 67613, 1998)
- ○ HOME FOR CHRISTMAS (RCA / BMG 67726, 1998)
- ○ NO STRINGS ATTACHED (RCA / BMG 69767, 2000)

~ 40 ~
The Eurovision Song Contest

The Eurovision Song Contest is the venerable elder statesman of modern pop. Other institutions may be older, others maybe better respected, others might be better known (at least in America), but can any other event in the musical calendar point not only to 45 years of unbroken service and growth, but also to as many years of international success, both as a spectacular in its own right and as the testing ground for some of the world's best loved entertainers?

Celine Dion, ABBA, Gigliola Cinquetti, Dana, Nana Mouskouri, Francois Hardy, Udo Jurgens, Julio Iglesias, the New Seekers, Patrick Juvet and Ofra Haza are just a handful of the names to have risen to international attention following Eurovision and, while the competition's name has seldom invoked much more than a stomach-clutching gurgle of pain from the average "serious" music fan, it's a whey-faced curmudgeon indeed who has gone through life utterly immune to the charms of the annual circus.

The tenets of the Eurovision Song Contest are simplicity itself. Staged annually by the European Broadcasting Union (EBU), who in turn took the idea from the San Remo Song Festival, member nations take to the field armed with what has been adjudged the best song they've got (drawn from a pool of volunteering songwriters, then whittled down through both committee and public votes), descending upon the host venue for one May evening of non-stop music. In the early days, barely a handful of countries entered. In the year 2000, 24 nations (out of the EBU's 40+ members) competed in an event which devoured four solid hours of prime time television across Europe.

The voting, until the late 1990's, was undertaken by sequestered committees in each competing nation — they would be contacted via satellite link (or before that, telephone) and asked to give votes for their ten most favored songs, home country excluded. More recently, home viewers have been polled, phoning in to register their own votes. Either way, national prejudices effortlessly leech out of the figures — the Scandinavian nations generally give full marks to each other; so do Greece and Cyprus. although neither like to vote for Turkey. Britain, France and Germany have a mutual exclusion zone all of their own, and it's telling that the countries which have proven the most successful over the years — Ireland, Luxembourg and Israel included — are those which have no other natural enemies within the voting bloc.

The competition rules are similarly basic. Since 1975, songs have had to be performed in a country's native or major language — one reason why so many songs rely on onomatopoeic "bing," "bong," "boom" and "bang" type lyrics. But as far back as 1968, Spain entered a song whose lyrics included the word "la" 138 times, three of them in the title. In 1982, Ireland squeezed in 111.

A song cannot have been entered before (hence Cyprus' late withdrawal from the 1999 competition — nobody noticed they'd already lost with the same ditty once before.) And whoever wins one year has to host the competition the next (although Monaco refused in 1972.) And that's about it — which means the other rule which many viewers believe to be immutable is, in fact, an absolute myth. Nowhere in the Eurovision law book is it stated that a performer has to come from the country he or she is representing.

Past non-European winners thus include an American (Katrina And The Waves — UK, 1997) and a French-Canadian (Celine Dion — Switzerland, 1989), while Australians Johnny Logan and Olivia Newton-John and Indian Cliff Richard (he was born in Lucknow, albeit to English parents) have also appeared.

Other unlikely victors have included an Israeli trans-sexual (Dana International, 1998) and two Norwegians, Bobbysox, whose triumph in 1985 came just seven years after their homeland equaled a 14 year old Eurovision record for the least number of points ever accrued by a competing song — absolutely none (the previous recipient, 1964's German effort *Man Gewohnt Sich So Schnell An Das Schone* simultaneously took the award for the longest title ever entered for the contest.) Since that time, the humorously-coveted "nul points" has become fairly common — Norway have grasped it on two further occasions; Finland, Germany, Switzerland, Holland, Spain and Austria head the list of other recipients.

There is no surefire recipe for victory. In 1967, the UK finally tired of scraping into (at best) the runners-up position ("we invented pop music after all, damn it") and unleashed chart-topping songbird Sandie Shaw on the quaking Euros. And she won. But when Cliff

Richard went to bat the following year, he came in a depressing second and, while Lulu took top honors in 1969, she had to share the trophy with no less than three other nations (Spain, France and Holland) without a recognizable name between them.

Pre-Eurovision fame, then, is no guarantee of victory. It's the song that counts, the sound and sometimes, the sentiment. It's probably no coincidence at all that in 1990, as Europe itself prepared for the seismic jelly roll of political and economic unification in 1992, Eurovision should be conquered by a group of Italians carousing, "Unite, 1992." Neither were too many observers surprised when, following ABBA's 1974 triumph with the mighty *Waterloo*, the next few years' events should overflow with ABBA look-alikes, Britain's coquettish Brotherhood Of Man included.

Other fashions, however, have found it notoriously difficult to penetrate the Eurovision veneer. In 1977, British punk band The Fruit Eating Bears made it to the UK regional finals and promptly finished last. Seven years later, "Wreckless" Eric Goulden might have journeyed at least as far with his own song for Europe, *Sugar Dick A Dum Dum*, but never got round to entering it.

On a less theoretical (and, if the truth be told, less satirical) level, 1980 found Belgian synthi-poppers Telex finishing last at the main event, with a quirky ditty quite coincidentally titled *Euro-Vision*. No attempts to stack the deck there. And in 1987, another name from the new wave archive, Plastic ("Ca Plane Pour Moi") Bertrand, plumbed equally ignoble depths when he tried relaunching his career trilling *Amour Amour* in a bright pink outfit which proved considerably more memorable than the song itself.

Neither is persistence necessarily a virtue. German songwriter Ralph Siegel has co-written a dozen Eurovision entries, nine for his own country, three for Luxembourg. Just one has won, 1982's *Ein Bisschen Frieden*. Italy's Gigliola Cinquetti triumphed in 1964, but finished an unlucky runner-up (unlucky because she was up against ABBA) a decade later; and, of course, Cliff Richard proved that lightning can indeed strike twice when he finished with the runner's up spot again in 1973. But there is always one exception to every rule — Ireland's Johnny Logan won the Grand Prix twice, in 1980 and again in 1987.

The greatest Eurovision entries, then, are the one-offs. Riva brought Eurovision triumph to Yugoslavia in 1989, thus ensuring that the 1990 event in Zagreb would be the last major event staged in that luckless nation before first, civil war, and then NATO self-aggrandizement tore it to ribbons. Yugoslavia itself arranged another first in honor of the occasion, a set of postage stamps celebrating Eurovision.

Then there were Israel's Lazy Bums (1987), whose Blues Brothers-esque routine ranks among the most delightful moments in 80's Eurovision history, but caused the country's Minister of Science & Development to resign in protest, describing the song as "an insult to our national intelligence." Plus ca change: six years previously, an entire country resigned, after Frenchman Jean Gabilou's *Humanahum* was beaten out of first place by UK ABBA clones Buck's Fizz. France announced an immediate boycott of the event on the grounds that the contest was "a monument to drivel and mediocrity." They subsequently returned, but have not noticeably set a higher standard.

Other treasures abound. Turkish superstars MFO's *Di Dai Dai Dai* (1986) returned to the headlines a decade later, when rocker Peter Murphy recorded a cover version of another song from the band's then-current album. There was Clodagh Rodgers, whose performance of *Jack In The Box* (1971) was so impassioned that her hair appeared to be on a spring of its own. There was Nicole (1982), memorably condemned by a bitter beaten competitor as "a fat German virgin with a big ass." And there was the 1980 Norwegian entry whose lyrics translated into an ode to a proposed hydro-electric power station. But finest of them all, the Swedes Holm and Tornell not only had a great song (*E' De' Det Har* — 1986), they also put on a tremendous stage show, co-starring a young girl in a maid's outfit, and a shirtless, sweaty, aging guitar god at whose feet the other performers swooned.

It's true, of course, that little about Eurovision invites comparison with any of the music industry's other gauges of talent and accomplishment — even a well-won Grand Prix will never compete with a Grammy or a Juno; holds none of the allure of a big hit single or a shiny gold record; is, in fact, little more than what its detractors say it is, an awfully long, awfully overblown smorgasbord of generally unknown singers screeching generally unmemorable songs, in front of what often looks like a generally unimpressed audience.

EUROVISION SONG CONTEST / LAUSANNE – SWITZERLAND 1989

Even the UK's decision to appoint an arbiter of national Eurovision taste, Jonathan King, paid only fleeting dividends, with victory in 1997. Famously stating that his ideal entry would be, "a 16 year old mixing jungle music in a bedroom in Ipswich and an imaginary housewife from Belfast writing a three minute operatic aria," King has since presided over his country's most dismal run ever — in 1999, Precious became only the second UK entry ever to finish outside of the top twelve (like Rikki in 1987, they came 13th.) In 2000, Nicki French hit a fresh all time low of 16th.

Still, Eurovision remains enshrined in the European psyche, a monument to so much that is great about modern pop music that its own failings fade into utter insignificance. Terry Wogan, since 1972 the British BBC's Eurovision compere, explains, "Eurovision is such a strange mixture of musical tastes and fashions. It has little relevance to popular music in this country . . . but [people] have been saying it won't survive for 20 years or more. Everyone's been writing it off. But the beast won't lie down."

Eurovision Song Contest Winners 1956-2000

1956	(Switzerland)	Lys Assia — *Refrain*
1957	(Holland)	Corry Brokken — *Net Als Toen*
1958	(France)	Andre Claveau — *Dors Mon Amour*
1959	(Holland)	Teddy Scholten — *Een Betje*
1960	(France)	Jacqueline Boyer — *Tom Pillibi*
1961	(Luxembourg)	Jean-Claude Pascal — *Nous Les Amoureux*
1962	(France)	Isabelle Aubret — *Une Premier Amour*
1963	(Denmark)	Grethe & Jorgen Ingemann — *Danevise*
1964	(Italy)	Gigliola Cinquetti — *Non Ho L'eta*
1965	(Luxembourg)	France Gall — *Poupee De Cire, Poupee De Son*
1966	(Austria)	Udo Jurgens — *Merci Cherie*
1967	(UK)	Sandie Shaw — *Puppet On A String*
1968	(Spain)	Massiel — *La La La* (three others finished with equal points — UK, France and Holland)
1969	(Holland)	Lennie Kuhr — *De Troubadour*
1970	(Ireland)	Dana — *All Kinds Of Everything*
1971	(Monaco)	Severine — *Un Banc Un Arbre Une Rue*
1972	(Luxembourg)	Vicky Leandros — *Apres Toi*
1973	(Luxembourg)	Anne Marie David — *Tu Te Reconnaitras*
1974	(Sweden)	ABBA — *Waterloo*
1975	(Holland)	Teach In — *Ding A Dong*
1976	(UK)	Brotherhood Of Man — *Save Your Kisses For Me*
1977	(France)	Marie Myriam — *L'oisueau Et L'enfant*
1978	(Israel)	Izhar Cohen & The Alphabeta — *A-Ba-Ni-Bi*
1979	(Israel)	Gali Atari & Milk & Honey — *Hallelujah*
1980	(Ireland)	Johnny Logan — *What's Another Year*
1981	(UK)	Bucks Fizz — *Making Your Mind Up*
1982	(W Germany)	Nicole — *Ein Bisschen Frieden*
1983	(Luxembourg)	Corrine Hermes — *Si La Vie Est Cadeau*
1984	(Sweden)	The Herreys — *Diggi Loo Diggi Ley*
1985	(Norway)	Bobbysocks — *La Det Swinge*
1986	(Belgium)	Sandra Kim — *J'aime La Vie*

1987	(Ireland)	Johnny Logan — *Hold Me Now*
1988	(Switzerland)	Celine Dion — *Ne Partez Pas Sans Moi*
1989	(Yugoslavia)	Riva — *Rock Me*
1990	(Italy)	Toto Cutugno — *Insieme 1992*
1991	(Sweden)	Carola — *Fangad Av En Stormvind*
1992	(Ireland)	Linda Martin — *Why Me?*
1993	(Ireland)	Niamh Kavanagh — *In Your Eyes*
1994	(Ireland)	Paul Harrington & Charlie McGettigan — *Rock'n'Roll Kids*
1995	(Norway)	Secret Garden — *Nocturne*
1996	(Ireland)	Eimear Quinn — *The Voice*
1997	(UK)	Katrina And The Waves — *Love Shine A Light*
1998	(Israel)	Dana International — *Diva*
1999	(Sweden)	Charlotte Nilsson — *Take Me To Your Heaven*
2000	(Denmark)	Brothers Olsen — *Fly On The Wings Of Love*

Eurovision Song Contest — UK Entries

1956 [no entry]
1957 Patricia Bredin — *All* . . . . (7th)
1958 [no entry]
1959 Pearl Carr & Teddy Johnson — *Sing Little Birdie* . . . . . (2nd)
1960 Bryan Johnson — *Looking High High High* . . . . (2nd)
1961 The Allisons — *Are You Sure* . . . . (2nd)
1962 Ronnie Carroll — *Ring A Ding Girl* . . . . (4th)
1963 Ronnie Carroll — *Say Wonderful Things* . . . . (4th)
1964 Matt Monroe — *I Love The Little Things* . . . . (2nd)
1965 Kathy Kirby — *I Belong* . . . . (2nd)
1966 Kenneth McKellar — *A Man Without Love* . . . . (9th)
1967 Sandie Shaw — *Puppet On A String* . . . . (1st)
1968 Cliff Richard — *Congratulations* . . . . (2nd)
1969 Lulu — *Boom Bang A Bang* . . . . (1st)
     (tied with Spain, France and Holland)
1970 Mary Hopkin — *Knock Knock Who's There?* . . . . (2nd)
1971 Clodagh Rodgers — *Jack In The Box* . . . . (4th)
1972 New Seekers — *Beg Steal Or Borrow* . . . . (2nd)
1973 Cliff Richard — *Power To All Our Friends* . . . . (2nd)
1974 Olivia Newton-John — *Long Live Love* . . . . (4th)
1975 The Shadows — *Let Me Be The One* . . . . (2nd)
1976 Brotherhood Of Man — *Save Your Kisses For me* . . . . (1st)
1977 Lynsey De Paul & Mike Moran — *Rock Bottom* . . . . . (2nd)
1978 Co Co — *The Bad Old Days* . . . . (11th)
1979 Black Ace — *Mary Ann* . . . . (7th)
1980 Prima Donna — *Love Enough For Two* . . . . (3rd)
1981 Bucks Fizz — *Makin' Your Mind Up* . . . . (1st)
1982 Bardo — *One Step Further* . . . . (7th)
1983 Sweet Dreams — *I'm Never Giving Up* . . . . (6th)

1984 Belle & The Devotions — *Love Games* . . . . (7th)
1985 Vikki — *Love Is* . . . . (4th)
1986 Ryder — *Runner In The Night* . . . . (7th)
1987 Rikki — *Only The Light* . . . . (13th)
1988 Scott Fitzgerald — *Go* . . . . (2nd)
1989 Live Report — *Why Do I Always Get It Wrong* . . . . . (2nd)
1990 Emma — *Give A Little Love Back* . . . . (6th)
1991 Samantha Janus — *A Message To Your Heart* . . . . . . (10th)
1992 Michael Ball — *One Step Out Of Time* . . . . (2nd)
1993 Sonia — *Better The Devil You Know* . . . . (2nd)
1994 Frances Ruffelle — *Lonely Symphony* . . . . (10th)
1995 Love City Groove — *Love City Groove* . . . . (10th)
1996 Gina G — *Ooh Aah . . . Just A Little Bit* . . . . (8th)
1997 Katrina & The Waves — *Love Shine A Light* . . . . (1st)
1998 Imaani — *Where Are You?* . . . . (2nd)
1999 Precious — *Say It Again* . . . . (13th)
2000 Nicki French — *Don't Play That Song Again* . . . . (16th)

Be sure to also look for: